Magazine
Photo Collage
A Multicultural Assessment and Treatment Technique

OTHER BOOKS BY HELEN B. LANDGARTEN

CLINICAL ART THERAPY
A Comprehensive Guide (1981)

FAMILY ART PSYCHOTHERAPY
A Clinical Guide and Casebook (1987)

Ed., with Darcy Lubbers
ADULT ART PSYCHOTHERAPY
Issues and Applications (1991)

Magazine Photo Collage

A Multicultural Assessment and Treatment Technique

Helen B. Landgarten, M.A.

Professor Emeritus, Founder, Former Director,
Graduate Department, Clinical Art Therapy,
Loyola Marymount University

Founder and Consultant, Art Psychotherapy,
Cedars-Sinai Medical Center, Family and Child Department
of Psychiatry, Los Angeles

Staff Research Associate,
Harbor University of California Los Angeles Medical Center,
Research and Education Institute

BRUNNER/MAZEL Publishers • NEW YORK

Library of Congress Cataloging-in-Publication Data
Landgarten, Helen B.
    Magazine photo collage : a multicultural assessment and treatment
technique / Helen B. Landgarten.
        p.   cm.
    Includes bibliographical references and index.
    ISBN 0-87630-706-3
    1. Photo collage – Therapeutic use.   I. Title.
RC489.P54L36   1993
616.89'1656 – dc20   93-16792
                                                                              CIP

Published by
BRUNNER/MAZEL, INC.
19 Union Square West
New York, New York 10003

Manufactured in the United States of America

10 9 8 7 6 5 4 3 2 1

WITH RESPECT AND GRATITUDE

to

Albertha Anderson and Martha Watson, who helped me better understand the pains and joys of the Black people.

The Molina family, because they shared their Hispanic lives and mores, and made me more aware of our commonalities and differences.

Leslie Ozawa, who taught me an understanding of the Asian culture's value system.

and

The many clients from various cultures who have enriched my knowledge and my life.

Contents

Illustrations

ASSESSMENT

TREATMENT

Foreword

Helen Landgarten's Magazine Photo Collage (MPC) represents a creative, culturally pertinent, flexible, and refreshing new treatment technique. The MPC is a long overdue effort to update and expand the classic but outmoded Thematic Apperception Test (TAT). The TAT involved a series of pictures to which stories were told. These pictures depicted Caucasians only. The MPC uses pictures cut from magazines representing Asians, Blacks, Hispanics, and Caucasians of all ages and sexes. Thus the MPC can be modified by the therapist to fit the particular population being treated.

The MPC is a technique all nondoctrinaire creative therapists will welcome as an extremely practical and useful treatment technique particularly appealing to intuitive or "right-brain" therapists.

I would have been aghast to review this work some 40 years ago. At that time I served as chief psychologist in a children's hospital and as a teacher of psychology in a medical school. My lectures to medical students regarding drawing techniques began, "The pencil or pen may be viewed as a stylus attached to the brain by the arm. The stylus moves on the paper and leaves marks as does the EEG or EKG. A skilled examiner may interpret these marks with as much scientific validity as the interpreter of the EEG or EKG."

My first published drawing technique, Kinetic Family Drawings (K-F-D) gave explicit instructions. The size of the paper and drawing tool were specified. The K-F-D was designed as a scientific tool that obtained a repeatable recordable drawing. Those standardized instructions and procedures for obtaining a K-F-D resulted from my left-brained training and my knowledge of the TAT.

Over the years I lectured to therapists using art in healing. Few of these students would conform to my left-brained K-F-D instructions. These right-brained artists would use any size paper they wished and any drawing tools. Instructions would vary or be ignored. I could not teach those right-brained therapists to become left-brained scientists.

Over the years I realized these right-brained artists did not view the pencil as a stylus. It seemed they viewed the drawing instrument as a magic wand opening up vistas of the unconscious and the intuitive. These artists refused to become linear and refused to worry about the reliability and validity and statistical repeatability so important to the scientist.

As an old left-brained trained scientist working in the field of art psychology I am appalled at the lack of progress or innovations in this field by "traditional" art psychologists.

In viewing this field from a 40-year perspective, I am reminded of the Greek story of Arachne, a skilled spinner and weaver transformed into a spider by jealous Athene. Arachne was condemned to useless and eternal spinning. "Spider" is derived from the root "to spin."

Left-brained linear "scientists" remind me of statistical spiders weaving webs of statistical information around techniques such as the MMPI and Rorschach observing the original vision and contributing no new information. Landgarten is no spinner and is not obsessed with statistical validity and reliability. She offers a magic box housing a myriad of pictures. One may take "four or five or six pictures" from the magic box and tell magical tales.

Despite my admiration for Landgarten's innovative MPC technique and for her as a pioneer magician in the world of art therapy, I cannot refrain from a few left-brained observations about the MPC. The MPC gives four tasks which when summarized are:

Task One: "Tell me anything that *comes to your mind* about each picture."

Task Two: "Write or tell what you imagine each person is *thinking* and what he/she is *saying*."

Task Three: "Pick out four, five, or six pictures that stand for something *good* and something *bad*."

Task Four: "Pick out ONE picture from the people box and write or tell what is *happening* to that person."

As the MPC grows one hopes a fifth task can be added: "What are the *feelings* involved?"

Serious therapists using the MPC may wish to review the original TAT technique and procedures. In essence the TAT called for a three-part story from each card, i.e., a beginning, a middle, and an end. Analysis of the story called for: 1) identification of a central figure in each story; 2) instigators and recipients of actions; and 3) needs and presses in each story.

The MPC has some pictures and stories with animals as central figures. For those interested in animal pictures they might review:

1. *The Children's Apperception Test* (CAT): (Bellack and Bellack) There are 10 pictures in the CAT consisting of animal pictures that depict many problems of childhood including feeding conflicts, sibling rivalry, toilet training, etc. The authors claim that children (ages 3 to 11) can identify more clearly with animals than with persons.
2. *Blacky Pictures*: Consists of pictures of dogs on the basis of which stories are told. The cards are drawn to canvass situations in Freudian theory to be related to psychosexual development.

The MPC has many other valuable, innovative techniques such as positive life reviews and positive memories.

Much progress in this field came from a synthesis of right- and left-brain variables. Freud was a neurologist whose interest in the unconscious brought science and intuition together. With this synthesis Freud was able to communicate with a large population. Carl Jung was a physician fascinated with the intuitive and the unconscious. His synthesis appealed to a wide audience. The major contributions of Freud and Jung came not from their left-brained "theories" but from their right-brained metaphors and techniques such as a free association and intuitive Mandala interpretation.

I was surprised when a magical right-brained author asked a more linear left-brained author to review her book. The task proved a useful and challenging one for me. Perhaps others will follow Landgarten in asking left-brained people to review their right-brained books and right-brained people to review left-brained books. Many of us could benefit from such a bridging.

In *Magazine Photo Collage,* a sensitive, experienced, innovative clinician takes you on a magical journey demonstrating the usefulness of MPC with a wide variety of clients of many ethnic heritages. Landgarten demonstrates the practical use of the MPC with a minimum of theorizing and a maximum of practicality.

Robert C. Burns
Director
Seattle Institute of Human Development

Preface

Mental health financial aid on the federal, state, and county level has been repeatedly cut. For economic reasons, a great many agencies have shortened their assessment and treatment time. Therapists in private practice have also been affected by reductions in insurance for mental health outpatient services. Consequently, tools that can hasten or aid the therapeutic process are constantly being sought.

This book focuses on a technique that can be used by clinicians from various mental health disciplines, including psychologists, psychiatrists, social workers, and marriage and family therapists and counselors. Although most art therapists are knowledgeable about the pictorial collage method, they, too, may glean some new ideas for its use.

The attraction of integrating Magazine Photo Collage (MPC) into the reader's style of working is that it is simple for the therapist to administer and for the client to produce. This mode is an inexpensive tool for aiding assessment and treatment.

A major advantage of the MPC is that it is *not culture-bound.* Unfortunately, the vast majority of projective tests that contain pictures of people have been designed to suit American Caucasian individuals. Black, Hispanic, Asian, American Indian, and other minority group persons have been measured against standards that may not be valid for their particular cultures. Because of the bias of current standardized methods for evaluation and intervention, the MPC augmentation provides a valuable new tool that may be used in tandem with projective tests that have been empirically validated.

This text gives the reader a mechanism that offers *ethnic versatility.* Both theory and application described in these pages may be used to any extent that the clinician finds beneficial. Experienced therapists will find that it complements their current style of practice. The novice is warned that this technique is *not meant to be a total way of working,* unless there is a specific reason for such a direction. The MPC provides the reader with an additional source for gathering assessment information and supplies an innovative intervention technique that is multicultural in nature. Hopefully, it will find a place in the therapist's armamentarium.

Acknowledgments

My deep gratitude to Jeffrey Lulow, Ph.D., for his encouragement and most valued suggestions. I am indebted to him for the time and effort he put into reviewing and commenting on my manuscript.

To Bernard Mazel, I extend my thanks, not only for editing this book but for giving me my first publication opportunity in 1980. Also, to my editor, Natalie Gilman, whose interest and availability sustained me during my last two books, as well as this current book.

Julie De Rose's enthusiasm about this text, and her contribution as a reader, is much appreciated.

Magazine
Photo Collage
A Multicultural Assessment and Treatment Technique

CHAPTER 1

Introduction and Theory

Numerous professional publications have discussed the subject of magazine photo collage. Yet, there is no textbook that is specifically dedicated to the reasons for its use and the applications of this technique.

For over 25 years, I have gathered information on the collage mode. Depending upon each individual case, I have utilized this media to varied degrees: a few times, or intermittently, or on rare occasion as the major form of treatment. It has demonstrated its value in my work both with children and adults of all ages. The MPC (Magazine Photo Collage) is beneficial during the assessment and treatment phases of therapy because clients can identify with the images and voice their projections onto their self-selected pictures.

A major problem that currently exists in the majority of projective tests is that they are *culture-bound* by their slanted Caucasian-American design. Assessment scores may be invalid for minority persons. Recently, the TEMAS (Tell Me a Story) test was developed by Constantine, Malgady, and Rogler (1988) to promote valid projective testing for Hispanic children. The environment in the TEMAS is urban, with images of children outdoors and in home situations. Boys and girls are shown alone, with peers, and in a family situation. The authors believe their pictures are more valid for the Hispanic subjects since they relate to the child's own ethnic lifestyle. The TEMAS Test is a step toward rectifying the problem of inappropriate testing procedures for minority school-age children. With the large influx of immigrants, this problem is presently acute.

A vital benefit of the MPC is that it can be administered to persons from any group since is not culturally biased. It can be matched to the clients' ethnicity *providing the therapist makes a point of including pictures that the client can relate to.*

Diligent clinicians who take the time to present magazine photos that represent the clients' culture will find that the therapy is enhanced.

The collage mode is a meaningful tool for the discovery of problem areas. Clients' conflicts, defense mechanisms, and styles of functioning are revealed in a short time.

The information presented in this book has not been validated by an empirical study. Suggestions or interpretations are based on my many years of clinical practice. This book does not lay claim to exact meanings for particular images. In fact, images can represent different meanings to different clients.

During the assessment phase, in a manner similar to the Thematic Apperception Test, the collage focus is on *content*. However, a feature that contrasts with many standardized projective tests is that here the collections of pictures is not always the same. The boxes of photographs contain a large number of magazine pictures that have been randomly chosen by the therapist and may differ from one session to another. Thus, probable responses are unavailable. It is essential, therefore, for the therapist to note pictorial elements as well as thematic configurations that are repeated by the client.

It is important for the reader to understand that a picture alone does not tell an entire story. One must gather the client's free associations to glean some understanding of the symbolism being presented. For instance, the therapist can assume that a photo of a crying person is related to the emotion of sadness. Yet, the underlying meaning of the image is of little worth without additional data. During the treatment phase, questions should be asked of the client. For example: What kind of person is this? Why is he or she feeling sad? What caused this feeling? What might happen to her/him in the future? What can help this person?

Because clients choose their own collage images, they are provided with a rich symbolic vocabulary for self-expression, and one that is individualized to suit their own needs. The opportunity to exercise some *control* over the selection process can lessen inhibitions and resistant factors for many clients. This facet also encourages the positive transference and hastens the establishment of a therapeutic alliance.

The MPC requires the clinician merely to tear or cut out pictures from magazines. Its casual appearance is an asset, as it is less formal than the usual set of printed images used in standardized projective tests. Clients are less threatened when they take the MPC for assessment or treatment.

Therapists will adjust this modality to fit into their usual approach to therapy. For those practitioners who administer projective tests, this mode can be easily combined with their current style of testing.

The four-task assessment protocol set forth in this book is simple to administer. During the treatment phase, when gliding from one task to another is required, greater skill is necessary. Continual thought must be given to the aims of therapy with instructions fashioned toward that end. Once again, readers are reminded to think in symbolic terms that match their customary form of treatment.

The MPC can be integrated into the *treatment process* very easily. At any point in therapy, it may be introduced through instructions for tasks that have a *thematic* orientation or a *free choice*. After the collage is completed, the clinician has several options: a) confronting the meaning of the pictures, b) making an intervention, c) offering an interpretation, d) noting yet skipping over the subject and going on to another collage. The decisions will depend upon the therapist's usual method of treatment.

Except for the assessment phase, therapists who normally use interrogations may continue in the same vein. For instance, regarding the "people images," the following questions may be asked: What kind of environment is that person in? How is that person feeling? What is making him/her that way? What is going to happen to him/her? What kind of person is he/she? Does that person have any alternative? What kind of family does the person have? How does he/she manage to cope with problems? Et cetera.

Regardless of the way in which the clinician proceeds, the client's collage *becomes the document* that gains access to conscious as well as unconscious material.

It cannot be emphasized too strongly that it is imperative for the clinician to understand her/his reason for turning to the MPC. Without such awareness, this modality is of little therapeutic value and, if incorrectly approached, may prove to be harmful. The reader should remember that it is requisite to steer instructions toward the objectives of each session.

It is critical for the practitioner to be aware that clients will expose unconscious material through the MPC. It may surface quickly, and without warning. The therapist must be alert to such an occurrence and, if it takes place, proceed with *caution*. One must avoid the urge to bring attention to the photo or to make an interpretation unless a therapeutic maneuver is clearly indicated.

In contrast to the verbal form of communication, the MPC is a metaphoric language of its own, one that clients can more easily tolerate and may use to gain a deeper understanding of themselves.

CHAPTER 2

Stimuli and Materials

The stimuli are magazine pictures. Therapists intentionally select photographs that are culturally homogeneous with their client population. The client's image familiarity makes the MPC a less intimidating assessment and treatment tool. Stimuli are presented in a somewhat casual way to diminish the client's self-conscious efforts and fear of being tested, and to allow greater freedom of expression for the individual.

STIMULI PREPARATION

The most effective stimuli preparation requires a collection of magazine photographs that are divided into two categories: one of PEOPLE, and the other of MISCELLANEOUS ITEMS. It is important to remove the printed words that may surround the images in order to evoke the client's own free associations, rather than letting them be influenced by the words connected to the pictures. In cutting or tearing out the images from the magazines, one must be careful to *avoid neatness*. The photos are far more effective when their appearance is not one of preciousness. In contrast to the standardized projective tests the casual pictorial presentation helps to alleviate some clients' self-exerted performance pressure.

Magazine pictures are placed into two different boxes, one that is labeled PEOPLE and the other MISCELLANEOUS ITEMS or THINGS. This type of photo separation is a significant time-saver, as several collages may be created and discussed in a single session.

PEOPLE PHOTOS

The PEOPLE photo collection should include the following:

1. A variety of persons from different cultures. The largest number should pertain to the therapist's client population.
2. The vast majority should be reality oriented, with only a few stereotyped glamorous pictures.
3. Male and female figures.
4. Persons of all ages.
5. A variety of facial expressions.
6. Movement and static body positions.
7. Varied economic conditions that display different walks of life.
8. Individuals placed in different types of environment.
9. Individuals who stand alone, are in dyads, are part of a group, or are in family settings.

Some therapists may wish to include portraits with eyes or ears that have been cut away. Such imagery may be shocking to some clients, yet will serve to elicit impressions that are symbolically indicative of themselves or of people they know.

If the client population contains several different minority groups, then be certain to also include photographs of those cultures. These images are a critical factor for effective evaluations and treatment. It is a disservice to deny clients pictures with which they can identify.

There are many magazines available in the ethnic communities that can be used for collage purposes. If the geographical location prevents the reader from gaining access to such magazines, refer to the reference list for names and addresses of some culturally aimed publications.

Magazines such as Life, Time, Newsweek, Sports Illustrated, National Geographic, Money, and Business Week, have pictures of minority group people under various conditions. Many advertisements now make a point of showing individuals from different countries. However, Hispanics are least available in most English-language magazines.

Pictures of men and women in pain or depressed present an affect that should be included in the collection. These images can often be found in drug company advertisements in medical and psychiatric journals.

Be certain that the MPC collection includes both black and white and color photographs. Unfortunately, color cannot be reproduced in this text. When black and white pictures are significantly used in the case histories described, this fact is noted.

MISCELLANEOUS PICTURES

The MISCELLANEOUS ITEMS collection should contain a large variety of photographs. If the therapist has a special agenda in mind, than images related to that goal may be planted in the box. For example, pictures that hint at: chemical or alcohol dependency; physical or sexual abuse; fire setting; eating disorders; suicidal ideation; guilt around parental divorce; repressed mourning; conflicting value systems; a delusional system, and so on.

Although the therapist may purposely select specific pictures for the MISCELLANEOUS ITEMS, it is extremely important that many images be randomly chosen. If this step is omitted, then the therapist's own projections may be exhibited and clients denied a chance to express themselves more fully.

The box of MISCELLANEOUS ITEMS is mostly filled with pictures from ads. Be certain to collect photographs from all types of magazines since ads are focused on the publication's reading population. For instance, a highly sophisticated magazine that features very expensive Vogue-like ads would be inappropriate for clients who are struggling to make a living.

Collect magazines and professional journals from other persons to add a different slant to the imagery. Additional publication purchases may be necessary to complete the photographic choices.

Most miscellaneous boxes tend to contain images of: clocks, trucks, cars, clothes, computers, dishes, furniture, tools, medicines, machinery, houses, animals, bottles of liquor, fires, plumbing, food, jewelry, scenes from nature. It is important to include pictures of trash, demolished homes, broken glass, guns, pills and other destroyed or broken fragile items. Since the items listed here are not an exhaustive list, therapists will use their own imagination to complete the pictorial collection.

It is advisable to have another person check over the image collection since the therapist's bias may be spotted. The reviewer may also make additional suggestions.

ADDITIONAL MATERIALS

1. Newsprint or any other type of white paper, size 16 x 20 is most useful.
   This size is especially desirable because it allows sufficient space for a number of pictures and can hold large images. It also provides greater space for the client's written statements.

   Newsprint paper is inexpensive and can be purchased in art supply stores or larger drugstores.
2. Colored construction paper may be used *after* the assessment phase. Color can be visually more inviting and may act as a task stimulus.
3. Two black felt nontoxic markers, one with a thin tip and the other with a medium sized tip.
4. A ball point pen.
5. Lead pencil with an eraser tip.
6. Two types of glue, liquid and stick. During the *first* assessment meeting, the milky type *liquid glue* (such as Elmer's or Wilhold) *is required*. The liquidity and squeeze bottle dimensions allow various ways of handling. It may be used precisely and adequately, or excessively and recklessly. For clients who use the liquid glue regressively, the more restrictive glue-stick medium is supplied in sessions that follow the initial meeting.
7. Rounded-tip scissors. The size depends on what is best suited for the client.
8. Masonite, a drawing board, or a piece of plastic approximately 26″ x 32″ to be placed on a desktop for protection. A folding table is an alternative.

CHAPTER 3

Assessment Administration

Before the MPC is administered for the assessment, the therapist proceeds with his/her standard approach to gathering the client's history. Data collected ahead of the MPC will give the clinician a better understanding of the possible personal meaning of some of the characters in the collage.

The therapist's stance while administering the MPC may differ from one clinician to another. This author finds it best to be seated and relaxed while making observations and taking mental notes, which are recorded after the client leaves. Practitioners who normally take notes during the evaluation procedure may continue with this style.

Before the client enters the office, the materials are set in place. These include: two collage boxes—one filled with people pictures and the other with miscellaneous items, four sheets of newsprint paper, liquid glue, scissors, two black felt markers (two tip sizes), lead pencil, and ballpoint pen.

The Four-Task Assessment Protocol should be adhered to as described herein.

The MPC procedure begins by informing the client that he/she is going to make a "Magazine Photo Collage." The therapist points out the contents of the PEOPLE box and the MISCELLANEOUS ITEMS. The latter can be called THINGS for children or adults who may not understand the word "miscellaneous."

Clients are told they will be choosing pictures from these boxes. The scissors can be used to trim or cut away parts of the pictures, or else the unwanted parts could be torn away, or the photos can be used just as they are. The liquid glue is for pasting the pictures onto the blank paper. The pencil or pen or felt markers are used for writing.

FOUR-TASK ASSESSMENT PROTOCOL

First Task

Instructions for the first task are: *Look through the box of* miscellaneous items *and pick out pictures that catch your attention. Paste them onto the paper.* The next instructions are: *Write directly onto the page, or tell me, anything that comes to your mind about each picture.* For children or illiterate persons, the therapist offers to take dictation. The directions may be given several times to insure that they are understood. Clients might need support to elicit and record or tell their free associations. For example, the therapist can encourage children simply by saying, "Most kids have fun picking out the pictures and making up something about them."

The *rationale* for the First Task is to begin the assessment by introducing an MPC that has the fewest instructions and is simple to master. In contrast to the next three tasks, it sets no boundaries on the number of pictures and allows greater freedom for the selection process. Miscellaneous pictures are requested because these are usually less threatening than those of people.

Attention should be paid to the following questions:

1. How are the photographs handled?
2. Were the images torn out, cut away, trimmed, or left in their original state before being pasted down?
3. How was the glue handled?
4. Was the placement carefully thought out, reasonable, or haphazard?
5. What was the gist of the pictorial content?
6. Did specific messages appear?

All of these points in composite convey information about the client.

Second Task

Instructions for the Second Task are: *Pick out four or five or six pictures of* people, *then paste them onto a second piece of paper.* The next instructions are: *Write or tell what you imagine each person is THINKING and what he/she is SAYING.*

If clients are hesitant about responding, encourage them to use their imagination by paying attention to the picture's facial expressions, or the body language, or the environment.

The *rationale* for the Second Task instructions is multifold. It reveals clients' perception about *trust*, regarding either themselves, someone in their life, or possibly the therapist.

The specified number of photographs is a way of observing reactions to limit-setting or to the authority figure. The reaction to this feature should be noted. Observe if the client chooses the lesser, correct, or larger amount of pictures specified in the instructions. If the number is within the designated range, note if it is the least, middle, or largest amount of photographs. Observations on the selection number are significant *only* if the next two tasks receive the same type of response. For instance, if the client always chooses less then the allotted amount, it might indicate a withholding feature, depression, or oppositional behavior. On the other hand, consistently exceeding the limit can hint at a rebellious attitude or difficulties with boundaries.

This second task also relates to the *congruencies* and *disparities* between what certain people THINK and SAY. Watch for the responses that different people make in the MPC. When there is a mixture of congruent and incongruent responses, then pay heed to the gender and age category of each figure. It is essential to note the characters in the photos who: 1) say what is on their mind; 2) hold back their thoughts either appropriately or inappropriately; 3) are devious or secretive.

Projections in this technique deal with clients' self-image, persons in their lives, and possibly the transference. Clients may or may not be aware of displaying their impressions of a parent, spouse, child, peer, employer, therapist, and others. Sometimes, a blatant resemblance between the photo and the symbolized person is seen.

Pictures are usually the same sex as their metaphor, except medical doctors, especially surgeons. These images, chosen unconsciously, often symbolize fantasies of problems being *cut out* or *fixed* by the clinician. If the therapist is a woman, then the sex of the doctor in the picture may not be matched. This may be due to a distancing mechanism, or simply because the people box did not contain such a photograph.

Third Task

Instructions for the third task are: *Pick out four, five, or six pictures from the boxes of* people *and/or* miscellaneous items, *that stand for something GOOD and something BAD. Paste them down and write or tell what the pictures mean.*

The *rationale* for the Third Task is to see what the person considers as GOOD and BAD. This reference is purposely left ambiguous. The vagueness is benign and nonconfrontive. Leeway is given in the choice since objects, persons, or situations can be selected.

Therapists should observe if only people, miscellaneous images, or a combination of both are presented. Generally, photos of people are more laden with emotion and deal with the self or relationships. Miscellaneous items are often used as a distancing mechanism.

Some clients choose humorous pictures from either collection, thus avoiding their feelings, hiding them, or testing the therapist's reactions. In these cases, an *interpretation is left unstated during the assessment procedure*, although it can be addressed during treatment.

Fourth Task

Instructions for the fourth task are: *Pick out only ONE picture from the* people *box and paste it down. The next direction is: Write or tell what is HAPPENING to that person.* Afterwards, ask, *Do you think the situation will CHANGE?* If the answer is "Yes," then instruct the client to *find a picture illustrating the change or tell WHAT will make it change.*

The *rationale* for the Fourth Task is to evaluate the person's positive or negative outlook. This will illuminate the individual's attitude, coping mechanisms, and whether or not problem-solving through alternatives is part of his/her life-style. If this last point is demonstrated, this strength will be pointed out and reinforced during the treatment phase of therapy.

If clients use humor for this task, their vulnerabilities are expressed in a joking manner. Pretense is put aside by the therapist, who can see beyond their disguise, and interpreted during treatment.

Comments. All four tasks, distanced from the client, are devised as a catalyst for the free association projections. They are designed to take up the time allotted for a single session. The therapist should judge whether the directive should be timed. If a time limit is set, then the pressure or frustration factor must be taken into account for the assessment.

If the client is allowed to pursue the tasks at a slow pace, the therapist must decide if the tasks are to be left incomplete or continued in the following meeting. Wherever possible, it is *advantageous for the entire MPC to be completed in a single session*.

CHAPTER 4

Assessment Procedure
Process, Pictorial Content,
Free Associations

The assessment process is divided into three parts: first, observing the client's approach to the task; second, viewing the pictorial content; third, gathering the written and/or verbal free associations. Although clues about the person may be gleaned from each of these steps, it is imperative that they are considered *in aggregate*.

Part I.
PROCESS: PROCEDURAL APPROACH TO THE TASK

The therapist's initial observation begins with the *way* in which the client approaches the collage procedure. The following points should *be viewed as a composite, with each part dependent upon the others*. Accordingly, it is paramount to gather the *gestalt* of how the person functions during the process. Note the following components.

1. The way that clients *look* through the box of pictures. Their attitude may be lackadaisical, serious, casual, disdainful, angry, anxious, et cetera.
2. The way the images are *handled*: recklessly, clumsily, adequately, casually, fastidiously.

3. Length of selection *time*: rapid, average, slow, extremely slow.
4. If or how the pictures are *trimmed or cut or torn*: recklessly, adequately, casually, efficiently, precisely.
5. The *gluing* style: extremely sloppy (including dripping and smearing), messy, adequate, casual, efficient, precise.
6. *Placement* on the page: haphazard (with overlapping images and pictures that go beyond the paper boundaries, for lack of space or in spite of existing room), sloppy, adequate, efficient, or exacting.
7. *Pictorial selection number*: excessive amount, within the limits, or a lesser amount.

As an example, there are clients who are *extremely cautious*: in selection decisions; cutting out or trimming around the images; the pasting method; pictorial placement. These persons may be any one or a combination of the following:

1. Passive as a way of dealing with resistance.
2. Depressed.
3. Ambivalent about revealing information or seeking treatment.
4. Unable to get in touch with or handle emotions.
5. Problematic in finding solutions or making decisions.
6. Obsessive-compulsive.

For instance, the obsessive-compulsive person would begin the procedure with a serious attitude, careful in handling the photographs and *cautiously slow* in decision making. The individual may make up secondary and tertiary sets of pictures—one for rejections, the other for possible acceptances. Selections stay within the limitations. After choices are made, the client may continue to be very neat in cutting out pictures and trimming around details (lack of time may prevent additional trimming). Considerable thought is given to placement before the pasting takes place. The glue is applied with care, and a pasting system is applied. If glue should happen to get onto the fingers, the person is fraught with disdain and immediately asks to wash their hands or wants a moistened tissue.

Individuals who exhibit these features are generally struggling to control their world. Their way of working is a mirror image of the way they function.

At the other extreme, there are clients who are *frantic* and work in *frenzied haste*. Photos are handled through grabbing gestures, some are crushed or ripped in a seemingly unintentional way. These individuals approach the task without giving it any thought. Attention is seldom paid to the limit-setting instructions. Although the instructions ask for four, five, or six pictures, their MPC may hold seven, eight, or more.

Rather than cutting away parts of the photographs, more often these clients tear or leave them in the original state. If cutting takes place, it is recklessly done. An excessive amount of glue is used, and the application and placement are slipshod. Even the limitation of page size does not adequately set boundaries for the collage. Some images are pasted one on top of another, with others hanging off the paper altogether. The entire MPC is created in a regressive fashion. Such a performance might be a clue to serious psycho-pathology. The following are possibilities:

1. Bipolar; manic stage.
2. Borderline personality, acting-out behavior.
3. Drug addiction.
4. Psychosis.

There are also individuals who *barely look* at the pictures and usually skip over many images. They may or may not be careless in the handling, gluing, and picture placement. If any cutting is done, it is sloppy and edges are not trimmed. Generally, the minimum number or a lesser amount of images is purposely selected as a way of testing the therapist. Resistance to the task is obvious. The nonverbal message is that the instructions were followed only to accommodate or symbolically "shut up" the therapist. Their contempt for therapy is usually displayed.

These clients are not proceeding with treatment out of their own choice. For various reasons, they have been coerced or ordered to receive treatment. Their passive aggressive mode of operating is a way of expressing their hostility.

There are other clients who look only at the pictures on the very top of the box. Their demeanor does not exhibit any resentment and they may be open to receiving therapy. What can be observed is their impulsiveness, along with an inability to delay gratification. These actions may be important hints that acting-out behavior may be a part of their lives.

Persons functioning at a high level will usually look through many images, but not necessarily all of them if the selection is generous. They handle the photographs in an average way. Their selection decisions are based on pictures that have an impact or eye appeal. The choices are made within a reasonable length of time—neither extra long nor recklessly quick. If pictures' edges are squared off, they are done so in a casual fashion. Some thought is given to placement and the photographs generally have space around each one. The amount of glue squeezed out is appropriate and does the job adequately. A finger may be used to smear the glue around the edges of the photos and is cleaned when convenient.

The following vignettes will further demonstrate what the therapist should look for as the client proceeds with the assessment tasks. Most typical examples at either end of the functioning continuum are demonstrated.

Procedural Illustrations — Process

John

John, a 22-year-old Asian male, was neatly groomed, intelligent, and functioning as a computer programmer. He sought therapy because of his anxiety. The client reported pride in his career accomplishments. He said that he would go over details time and time again, otherwise he "could not rest." John reported that management complimented him on the perfection of his work and his attention to details was outstanding. Consequently, he was shocked by his recent job layoff.

John understood that his supervisor had let him go because he was unable to meet the company's deadlines. Still he was puzzled by this action since he was very skilled. He professed that production work went against his grain. John believed it was critical that everything be checked, rechecked, and rechecked again, especially since quality control was an absolute necessity.

During the assessment procedure, John was extremely fastidious. He viewed and handled each magazine photo with care. In an orderly fashion, he set up two piles of pictures, one that was designated for rejections and the other for possible acceptances. The final choices were made only after he had looked over the images again.

The selected pictures were cut and trimmed with exactness. Liquid glue application was precise. Dots of glue were squeezed out and set in a particular pattern — one in each corner, then another one centered between. In a somewhat ritualistic fashion, this pattern was repeated on all the other pictures. Forethought was given to pictorial size for placement purposes to make certain that images were well balanced. John was careful not to get glue on his fingers, but when this occurred he promptly stood up and requested permission to go and wash his hands (Figure 1).

This extreme need to be cautious in decision-making and his striving for neatness and precision suggested that a compulsive feature was a part of John's

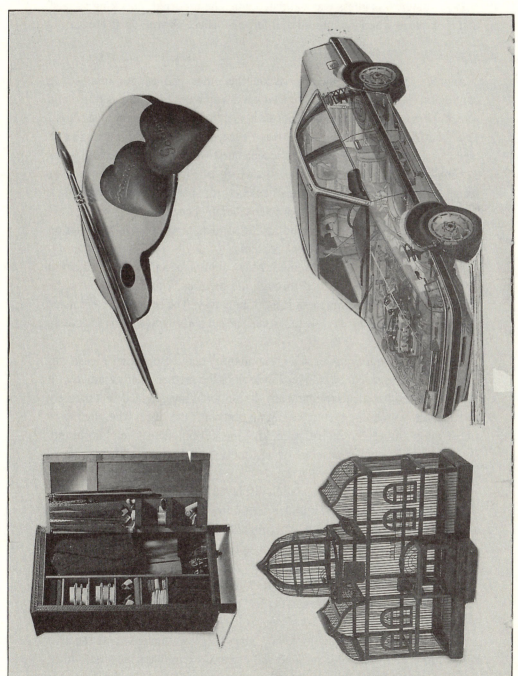

FIGURE 1

anxiety. Later, this guess was validated when he reported "checking rituals" that took place when he entered and left his office, as well as at home.

Mary

Another illustration, one that is on the other end of the functioning continuum, is Mary, an attractive Black woman in her mid-30s. A television screenwriter by profession, she reported herself to be at the "height of success." The client explained, "I can do no wrong, everyone recognizes I'm the greatest talent around." Mary described a recent burst of energy that proved to be extremely productive in her work. By chance, she happened to mention her recent spending sprees and some traffic tickets for speeding. She found herself "too busy to eat." Mary was motivated for therapy because of her weight loss. She wondered if taking "a workshop in stress management" would put her on "the right path" and alleviate her problems.

When the first task was presented, Mary approached the MPC project in a frenetic fashion. She hurried through the pictures with no regard for the photographs, often handling them in a crushing way. The selections were made in an off-hand manner. The few times that she cut parts away, it was recklessly done.

The glue was squeezed out in a great quantity and the pasting process was messy. Glue was smeared all over the back of the picture, getting much of it on the table and her hands (without any discomfort). Image placements grossly overlapped, with some pictures hanging partly off the page. The client was intent upon filling the entire page, making certain there were no empty spaces. Mary was either unaware or was not bothered by any of these features (Figure 2).

Looseness of the MPC presentation displayed the following features: a lack of structure, no boundaries, impulsiveness, low frustration tolerance. It was a good example of "acting-out art." In children's cases where similar characteristics are manifested, there is usually a tendency toward behavioral problems and/or learning disorders.

Mary's manic state was obvious and grandiosity a possibility. Yet, without examining the pictorial content and the free associations, even educated guesses were premature.

When the MPCs were completed, Mary's collage images and the free associations demonstrated: inflated self esteem, excessive sexual activities, a disenchantment with friends and relatives, and a zealous attitude toward her religious belief. Mary was evaluated as Bipolar in a Manic Episode. A medication consult was ordered, along with individual treatment.

FIGURE 2

PART II: PICTORIAL CONTENT

People Pictures

The second part of the MPC assessment aid is the examination of the pictorial content. Both inclusions and exclusions are noted. While observing pictures of *people*, one must pay attention to the following questions:

1. Are *all* of the photographs either of men or women, or of boys or girls?
2. Are the images generally mixed between males and females?
3. Is a certain age range consistently selected, or is there a diversity of ages?
4. Are most of the pictures the same age as the client or are they in the range of his/her parents or children?
5. What emotional expression is on the faces of the majority of people? Do they look sad, happy, angry, in pain, aggressive, or do they lack any affect?
6. Do particular emotions consistently appear on the faces of a particular sex?
7. Are the figures usually in isolation, paired, within a group, or part of a crowd?
8. Are the pictures entirely in black and white, even if most of the choices are available in color?

The photos in the MPC are: projections of the client's self, symbolic of significant persons in their life, and/or a transference statement. Although the MPC tends to be reality-oriented, there are times when images are used to represent wish-fulfillments.

The therapist's hypotheses may be validated or negated when the free associations are made. In addition to psychopathology, the individual's strengths can be seen. Such concrete evidence can be used as positive reinforcement during the treatment phase of therapy.

Miscellaneous Pictures

The MISCELLANEOUS ITEMS may disclose the person's value system, attitude toward life, concerns, fears, and wishes. Each image has a multiplicity of meanings, as they are indigenous to the client's stage of development. For example, a "car" for one child meant "I love my Daddy, he takes me for rides on Sunday." An adolescent said it stood for "my own wheels, so I can be free from my parents." An old man with a fatal disease claimed it was a metaphor for "getting ready for my final ride."

Although the vast majority of photographs appear benign, there are certain images that raise a red flag alert. These include: a looped rope, crashed automobiles, wrecked homes, cracked glass of any sort, knives, guns, or pills. Lethal or destroyed objects, especially if repeated, might reflect fragility, self-destructive ideation, or painful memories.

PART III: FREE ASSOCIATIONS

After information has been gathered through the procedural process and by the image selection, the *free associations* are critical to validate any type of theory or assumptions regarding the client.

Any of the client's verbal responses are acceptable. They may be in a single word or sentence, or several paragraphs long. The clinician's openness to the client's productions is essential. Otherwise, the client's attitude is affected and the selection process contaminated.

MPC ASSESSMENT ILLUSTRATIONS

Hispanic Nine-Year-Old Female: School Phobic

Clarita Ramarez was part of an intact family and the youngest of four children. The other siblings ranged from ages 12 to 16. Spanish was the only language spoken in the home.

The educational authorities were concerned about the child's frequent truancies. When Clarita was questioned about it, she merely answered with, "I don't know."

This issue was discussed with Mr. and Mrs. Ramarez, but they did not see it as a problem. They believed their daughter would outgrow it.

Despite the parents' opinion, the school psychologist insisted that the child receive treatment.

The first time Clarita entered the office she appeared shy and frightened. The MPC was explained to her and she was easily involved since she was attracted to the pictures. The statements on the collages were dictated by Clarita for the therapist to record.

First Task

The first task wording was simplified for the child. Clarita was instructed: *Look through the box with pictures of things and choose some. Paste them onto the white paper.* The next directions were: *Make up something about all of the pictures.*

The child was thoughtful about her pictorial selections. Her pasting and placement were reasonably done. Free associations were made with ease.

The MPC (Figure 3A) and the comments included:

1. The *carousel* reminded her of the "merry-go-round in Santa Monica."
2. *Eagle flying toward a mountainous rock* symbolized, "the bird's going home."
3. The *doll's head* received the remark, "It's a pretty doll," then she longingly added, "I wish I had a doll like that."
4. The *slipper made up of dollar bills* brought a smile as she said, "That's a funny shoe."

Comments. The *bird going home* seemed to hint at her school phobia. However, during the assessment phase questions were not asked. If it had occurred during treatment, the following inquiries would be made: Why was the bird was going home? What was happening at home? Who was in the house? How did the little bird feel? What is the mother bird like? The picture of the "bird" could be used after the assessment was completed.

Second Task

The second task was: *Pick out four, five, or six pictures from the box of people and paste them down.* Next, *pretend and tell what each person is THINKING, then what they are SAYING.*

Clarita made an effort to pick out enough images to tastefully fill the space. Her gluing and placement were adequate. However, the "thinking and saying" directive was apparently confusing.

The child merely made statements about each picture just as she had for the first task. No effort was made to point out the omission of "people's thoughts and sayings." Because the session was not to be associated with school, Clarita was allowed to complete the task in the way that she understood it.

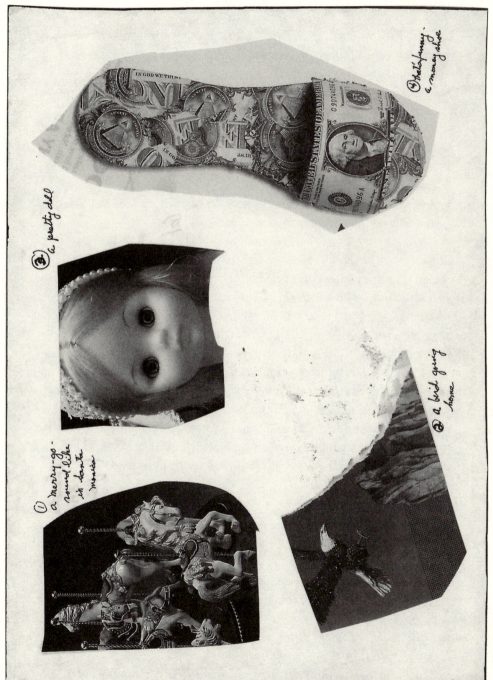

FIGURE 3A

The MPC included (Figure 3B):

1. *A teacher leaning over and touching two young Hispanic girls who were sharing a book* brought the comment, "The teacher is nice 'cause she helps the children to learn to read."
2. *A young Hispanic girl with her fingers in her mouth* brought the response: "The girl is worried about her mother."
3. *The head of a beautiful Hispanic woman* elicited, "The lady is pretty. She is happy."
4. *A woman with her mouth open* evoked the remark: "This lady doesn't feel so good."
5. *A Hispanic boy and girl* represented: "A boy who is nice to his sister." She added, "My brother is nice to me."

Comments. The child made an effort to create an attractive collage. Associations were particularly meaningful because Clarita purposely selected Hispanic pictures, with which she could identify. The MPC revealed that she liked her teacher and found her helpful, thus ruling out the school phobia because of a negative impression of the educator.

The photograph of the child who was worried about her mother was a meaningful clue. The information about the pretty woman who is happy, and the one who "doesn't feel so good" might refer to two of her mother's characteristics.

School phobic children are often in a symbiotic relationship with their mothers and worry about them when separated. For this reason, the child's truancy as a part of "separation anxiety" was seriously considered.

Third Task

The third task was: *Pick out four, five, or six pictures of people and/or things that show something GOOD and something BAD. Then talk about what the pictures mean.*

Clarita's pictures of GOOD and BAD things were set down (Figure 3C). The GOOD was portrayed through:

1. *Children with confetti falling on them* meant that "Disneyland is good."
2. A *doll* stood for "Playing with my doll is good."
3. The *statue of Virgin Mary praying* symbolized "Praying is good."

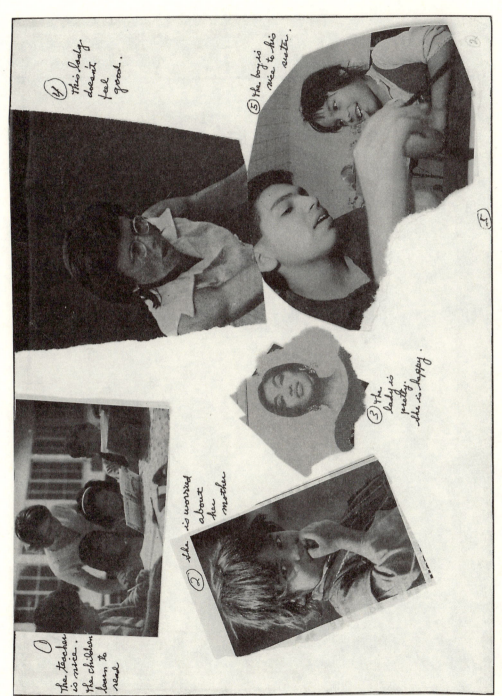

FIGURE 3B

FIGURE 3C

The BAD was portrayed through a single stark photograph of a *Hispanic woman's face* that was identified as "Bad is a lady who's worried. She's scared."

Comments. The "woman who is worried" comes up again. Its repetition lends more strength to the hints about concerns for her mother. The separation anxiety in relation to school phobia was further considered.

Fourth Task

The fourth task was: *Pick out only ONE picture of a person and paste it onto the page. Write or tell what you imagine is HAPPENING to that person.*

Clarita was very serious about this task. She took a great deal of time to find a photograph of a *contemplative woman standing on a bridge*. In answer to "What is happening to that person?" the child replied, "Maybe she'll fall. Maybe get hurt. She's sad" (Figure 3D).

The question was asked, "Will she stay sad or will things change?" Clarita quickly said, "Oh, she's gonna feel better." The child was directed to *pick a picture to show what will make the mother feel better*. She chose a picture of a *black woman in the kitchen baking, with a child alongside of her*. She explained, "This makes *my* mother feel better" (Figure 3E).

Comments. It is common for young children to pick out pictures that are directly related to family members. When this is done, it is not unusual for the child to slip into first person when explaining the images.

Clarita unconsciously shows that she sees her mother as depressed and fearful. She presents the "kitchen activity" as the way she helps to change mother's mood.

It was plausible that the mother may inadvertently cue her child into staying home from school to fend off her emotional state. Due to this parent/child dynamic, Clarita felt responsible for lifting her mother's depression.

As a check system, the MPCs were thematically focused on specific questions during the treatment phase. Clarita was instructed to pick out pictures on the following topics: 1) *What do you do with your mother when you stay home from school?* 2) *How does your mother feel most of the time?* 3) *What do you do when your mother is happy?* 4) *What do you do when your mother is sad?* 5) *How do you feel when you leave home and go to school?* 6) *What do you think about when you are not busy in school?*

Therapy recommendations were made. Clarita was to continue in individual treatment and her mother would also receive therapy.

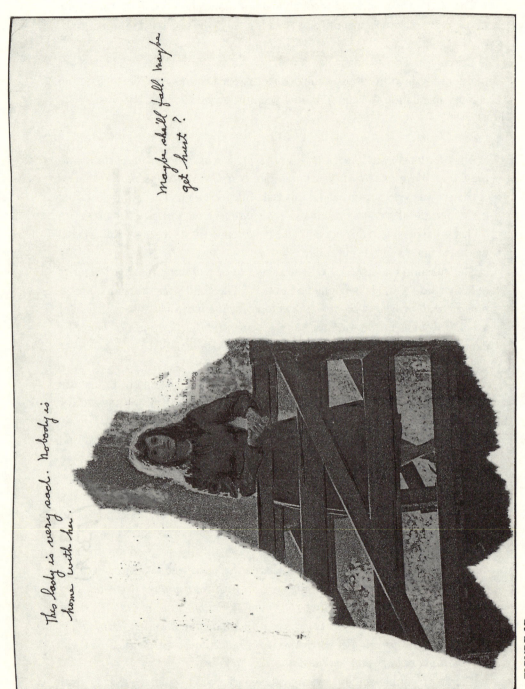

FIGURE 3D

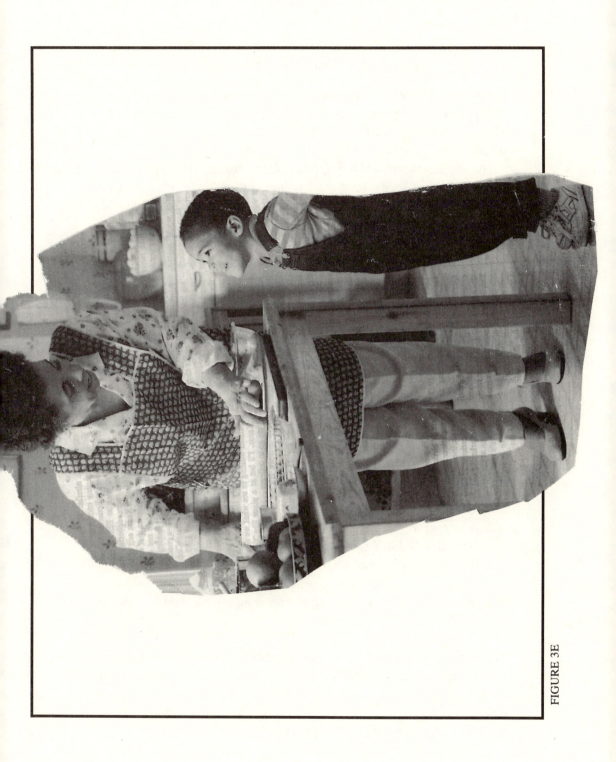

FIGURE 3E

Caucasian 15-Year-Old Female: Anoretic

Marla was somewhat plain, with a very thin body, neatly groomed, and with clothes that were color coordinated. Of the three daughters, the parents saw Marla as their only "perfect" child. They said she was a "lovely and a considerate person, always sensitive to everyone."

The adolescent was a highly gifted "model" student. Her past educational performance had always been outstanding. However, she had recently complained about being unable to concentrate in school. Because Marla was bothered by this inability, she agreed to therapy.

Despite her belief that she wanted help with her problem, Marla was resistant to divulging personal information and held back therapy progress. Consequently, the MPC mode was integrated into the classical approach.

First Task

The first task was: *Look through the miscellaneous items and pick out pictures that catch your attention. Paste them onto the paper. Next, write on the page or tell anything that comes to your mind about each picture.*

Marla, suspicious of the MPC procedure, gingerly fingered the photographs and took a very long time to make her final choices. She was neat in the way she applied the glue and placed the pictures.

The MPC (Figure 4A) included:

1. *The lower portion of a male figure wearing pants but no shoes is lifting up a bare-legged woman.* The photo was identified with the word LOVE.
2. *A carrot that formed a nose, with a pair of eyeglasses placed upon it* was labeled A NOSEY CARROT.
3. *A scale* was captioned UGH.
4. An ad for *Healthy Choice Frozen Food* went untitled.
5. *A bottle of Evian spring water with a nipple on the top* was labeled NATURAL.

Comments. The "nosey carrot" picture probably alluded to the therapist who wore glasses and would surely question her. The scale, accompanied by "ugh," seemed a lead to anorexia nervosa, especially since Marla was very thin. A typical symptom of this eating disorder is the person's unwillingness to grow up. This is demonstrated by the nipple-capped water bottle.

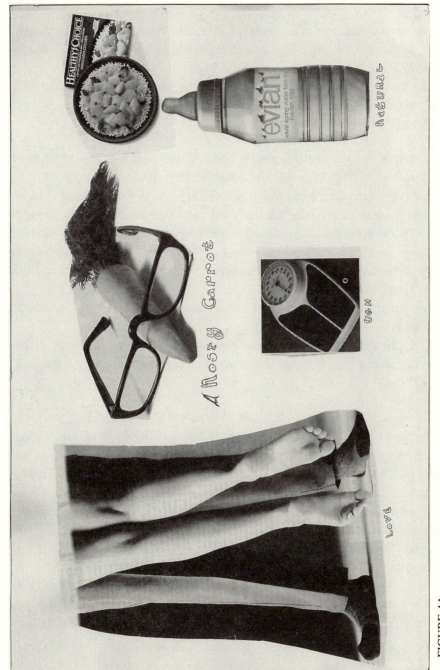

FIGURE 4A

Second Task

The second task was: *Pick out four, five, or six pictures from the people box and paste them onto the paper. Next, write or tell what each person is THINKING and what he or she is SAYING.*

The images were selected without hesitancy. Marla was fancy in the way she placed little circles around the "thinking" statements.

The MPC (Figure 4B) contained:

1. *A little Caucasian girl beautifully clothed* was thinking, "I'm 2 [*sic*] fat," but was saying, "Look at me, I hate this dress."
2. *Smiling little Caucasian girl with stacks of plates in front of her and about to eat corn on the cob.* She was thinking, "Yummy," and said, "Good."
3. *A forlorn Caucasian teenage girl holding a suitcase and a stuffed animal in one hand and a purse and tennis racket in the other.* The girl was thinking, "I'm going to college with my Teddy," while she said, "Good-bye!"
4. *A smiling little Caucasian girl with someone's arms around her,* was both thinking and saying, "I'm happy."
5. *A little Caucasian girl lying on her stomach with her face turned to the side, and a hand over her mouth* was thinking, "I got a secret," but asked, "What?"

Comments. The disparities between what people THINK and SAY is shown in the *food* related photographs (numbers 1 and 2). It points to information that is being withheld by Marla. This evidence is probably connected to the picture of the girl who thinks, "I've got a secret," but covers it up by innocently asking, "What?"

By viewing the build-up of *food* references from the first and second tasks, the additional data goes toward anorexia nervosa. More clues are gleaned from the joke "2" instead of "too." It betrays her body perception that she is big enough for two people. A classic example of the anoretic's ambivalence to grow up is typified in her picture of the girl who takes her suitcase and her "teddy bear" with her to school.

The girl with "a secret" seem to belong to Marla's hidden eating disorder.

Third Task

The third task was: *Pick out four, five, or six pictures of people and/or miscellaneous items that stand for something GOOD and something BAD. Paste them down and write or tell what the pictures mean.*

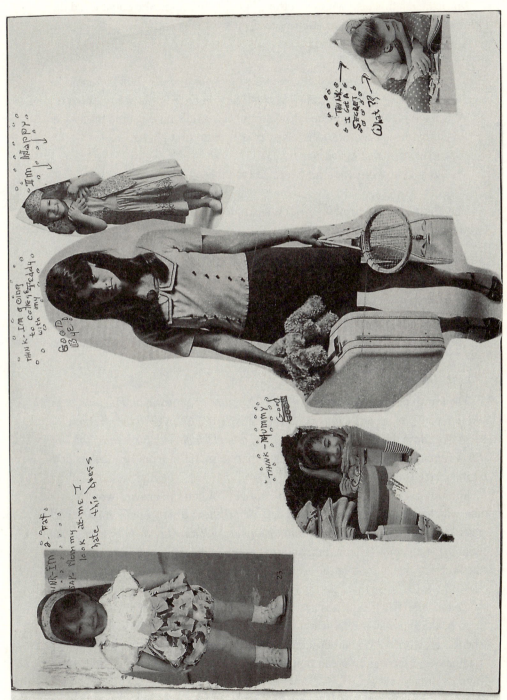

FIGURE 4B

Marla began this task with something specific in mind. She considered the gluing and placement in an attempt to do it well (Figure 4C).

The GOOD MPC included:

1. The *upper portion of a woman's body with a smile on her face.*
2–4. Two images demonstrated *women lying on their backs doing exercise.* Each picture is trimmed down to form a circle and become breasts as they are pasted onto the chest of a *woman* in a photo.
5. *A woman resting on her bike.*
6. A young woman on an exercise machine.

The BAD was presented through a single large-sized photo of a *pretty woman stuffing herself with cake.*

Comments. The eating disorder assessment continues as five of the GOOD images point to an obsession with weight loss. The formation of the "breasts" may again indicate either her perception that they are too large or the fear of growing up to have a bust.

The BAD photographs further emphasize her desires and fear of weight gain.

Fourth Task

The fourth task was: *Pick out only ONE picture of a person and paste it onto the page. Write or tell what you imagine is HAPPENING to that person.*

Marla chose the photo of the *top part of a man's face with his hands holding his forehead* (Figure 4D). She claimed that he suffered from headaches and stomachaches and was "*worried.*"

She was asked, *"Will the situation change?"* When the answer was "Yes," she was instructed: *Pick a photograph or tell how it will come about.* The response was an illustration of *a smiling woman cleaning up the bathroom sink,* with the statement, "Clean it up and feel good." She explained, it represented the worried man's motivation to "clean up his act."

Comments. The headaches and stomachaches often accompany the lack of food intake and may resemble her own symptoms. Like the man in the picture, she too is "worried" about her condition. The "cleanup" photograph contained a female and seemed to mean that Marla has good intentions to clean up her own dysfunctional act.

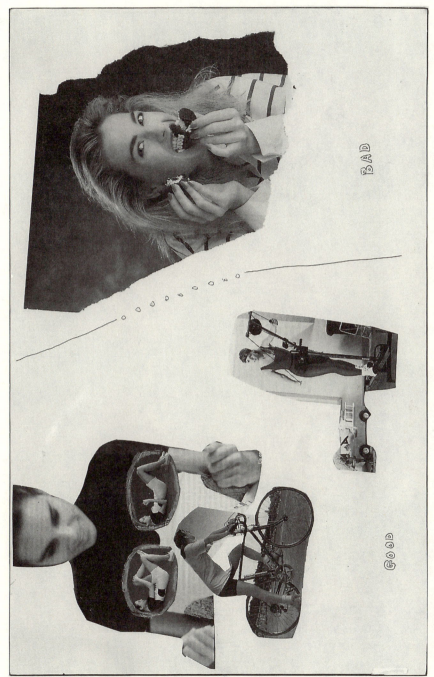

FIGURE 4C

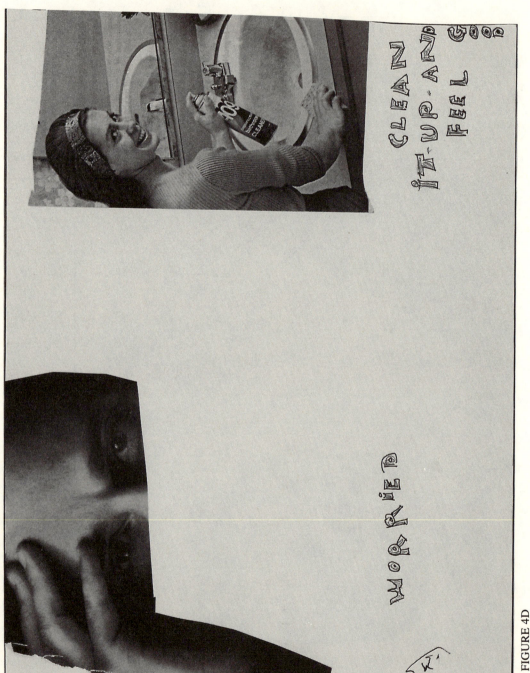

FIGURE 4D

Black 16-Year-Old Female: Unwed, Pregnant

Samantha was unwed and pregnant. With her family's support, she decided to keep her baby when it was born. She resented her physician's mandate that she receive therapy. He believed it was essential for Samantha to deal with the pregnancy, forthcoming delivery, and issues indigenous to an unwed teenager about to become a mother.

The client was openly hostile as the assessment procedure was explained. She was enraged at being expected to discuss personal matters with someone who was not only a stranger, but also not Black.

First Task

The first task was: *Look through the box of miscellaneous items and pick out pictures that catch your attention. Paste them down on the paper. Next, write on the page or tell anything that comes to mind about each picture.*

Although Samantha displayed her disdain, she realized that by picking out photos talk about herself could be delayed. She lingered and took a long time to make a selection, then dawdled before the images were pasted.

The MPC (Figure 5A) included:

1. The *rear-ended car with a "stop sign" in front of it* was associated with, "The car didn't pay attention to the stop sign so it got hit."
2. A *doll* was identified with, "I love dolls."
3. *Two hands about to shake. One is without a glove while the other is enclosed in a metal glove (similar to a knight's).* The remark about this image was, "The metal will keep the hand from getting hurt."
4. *Foggy snow-capped mountains* elicited the response, "It's a volcano."

Comments. An initial hint was the *injured auto that did not pay attention to the "stop sign."* It seemed to be symbolic of Samantha's lack of caution while having intercourse. Another hint was the *doll*, which indicated an unreadiness to grow up. The *mountain in the heavy fog,* identified as a "volcano," may have represented her own overflowing rageful feelings about her situation. Lastly, the *metal-gloved hand* appeared to be a transference image. It was possible that Samantha feared being squeezed too hard by the Caucasian therapist to reveal herself.

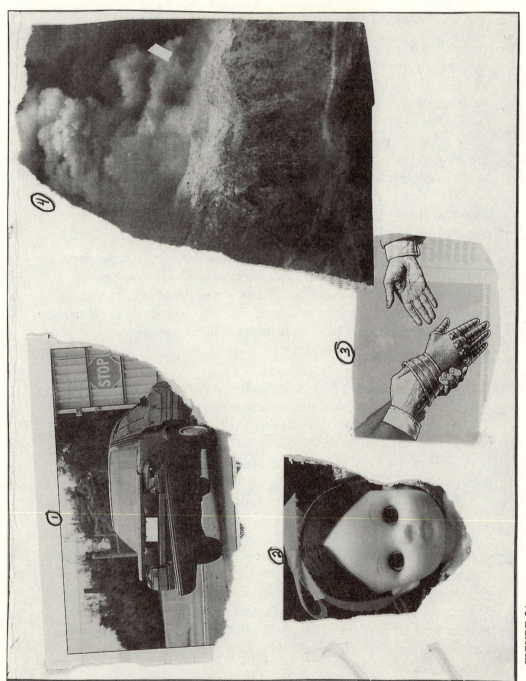

FIGURE 5A

Second Task

The second task was: *Pick out four, five, or six pictures from the people box and paste them onto the paper. Next, write or tell what each person is THINKING and what he or she is SAYING.*

Samantha passively took a long time to choose the photographs and very slowly pasted them down. Several images were left hanging off the page. The MPC (Figure 5B) included:

1. *An older Black woman holding a Black baby* was thinking, "I love this baby," and was saying, "You are a good baby."
2. *A black pregnant girl* was thinking, "I'm going to have a baby and I'm scared," while aloud she stated, "It's okay that I'm going to have a baby."
3. *A Caucasian doctor examining a baby* was thinking, "There is something wrong with this baby," yet he said, "The baby is healthy."
4. *A happy Black man laughing as he lies on a field of flowers* was thinking, "I'm happy," and declared, "Yo man! It's a great day."

Comments. The picture of the *Black woman* may have symbolized Samantha's mother, whose thoughts and words are congruent with her love and caring toward the future baby. The adolescent's fear of childbirth is veiled by a facade. This is evidenced through the *Black pregnant girl* picture with the dichotomy between what is being thought and said.

Samantha's apprehension is also evidenced through the photo of the *doctor* who is thinking that there is something wrong with the baby. Another interpretation might be that she does not trust what the therapist says.

There is some question about the metaphor of the *happy Black man*. He might represent the baby's father, her own parent, or some other male. It is altogether possible that this picture can simply be a compensatory wish for a boyfriend who is warm and caring about her situation. Regardless, without asking questions during the assessment procedure the identification of this man is incomplete.

After the assessment, this MPC would be brought out and used as a story-telling device.

Third Task

The third task was: *Pick out four, five, or six pictures of people and/or miscellaneous items that stand for something GOOD and something BAD. Paste them down and write or tell what the pictures mean.*

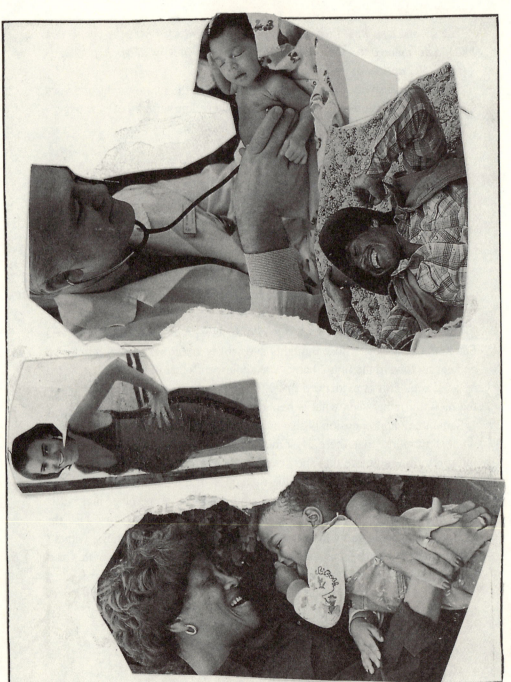

FIGURE 5B

While viewing the images, Samantha favorably commented on the large number of Black people photos that were in the collage box. It seemed that this feature put the therapist in a more positive light (Figure 5C).

The GOOD MPC included:

1. *A Black girl in a graduation cap and gown* represented, "getting a high school diploma."
2. *A Black man playing with a black baby* symbolized, "Having the baby's daddy around is important." This remark was made in an offhanded manner, as if it did not apply to her.

The BAD MPC contained only one picture.

1. *A Black baby in a coffin* was accompanied with the words, "a dead baby."

Comments. In this MPC, Samantha expressed her plans to finish high school and her wish to have the child's father available. Once again, she vented her fear that the baby might not survive. Perhaps it was due to some abortive act or fantasy, or simply a concern that is common among pregnant women. Later, during the treatment phase, this collage was also brought out and dealt with.

Fourth Task

The fourth task was: *Pick out only ONE picture of a person and paste it onto the page. Write or tell what you imagine is HAPPENING to that person.*

Samantha picked a *Caucasian runner* (although images of Black runners were available). She claimed that "The person was in a race." When asked, *Will he win or lose?* She replied, "I don't know" (Figure 5D).

Comments. Samantha may have picked a "Caucasian male runner" to distance herself from her own race with time until the baby is born. She repeated her anxiety when she claimed that she did not know if the runner was going to make it.

During treatment, hints that were included in this MPC were interpreted and explored.

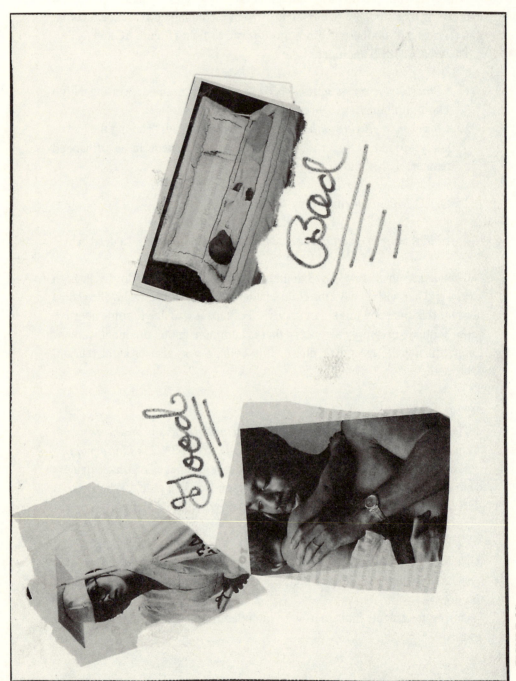

FIGURE 5C

FIGURE 5D

Asian 20-Year-Old Female: Bulimia Nervosa

Kim Misui suffered from bulimia. Her parents with professional careers were successful role models in their community. She attended a university and lived in a coeducational dormitory. During the semester break, Mrs. Misui discovered her daughter's gluttonous habit of overeating and then going to the bathroom to vomit out her food. It was at her parents' insistence that Kim entered therapy.

First Task

The first task was: *Look through the box of miscellaneous items and pick out pictures that catch your attention. Paste them onto the paper. Next, write on the page or tell anything that comes to mind about each picture.*

Kim enthusiastically busied herself by looking through the box of miscellaneous items. She was quick to pick out her pictures. Without any consideration being given to placement, they were pasted in overlapped positions.

The MPC (Figure 6A) included:

1–8. *Various pictures of food* received one label, YUMMY.
   9. *A woman holding a pair of dice* was accompanied by the title, THE GAMBLER.

Comments. Like most bulimics, Kim selected an abundant amount of "food" photographs for her MPC. The instructions for the selection of miscellaneous items only were ignored, as she impulsively included the picture of the female "gambler." Perhaps, this metaphoric image represented her risky bulimia or her gamble in making a commitment to therapy.

Second Task

The second task was: *Pick out four, five, or six pictures from the people box and paste them onto the paper. Next, write or tell what each person is THINKING and what they are SAYING.*

Kim's approach was similar to the first task. She was quick to ignore the directions and picked out a profuse number of images. A great quantity of glue was used and the picture placement was haphazard. Images overlapped and some extended beyond the edge of the paper.

FIGURE 6A

The MPC (Figure 6B) included:

1-7. *Obese women.* All of them were thinking, "I'm too fat, I hate the way I look," although they said, "I've got to go on a diet."

8-9. *Two obese men* received a remark about their "big belly." Both figures thought and said, "So I'm fat but I love my beer."

9-10. *Two slim girls on scales.* One was thinking, "It's working" and said, "That's better," and the other extremely underweight girl both thought and said, "Great!"

11. *A shapely yet faceless woman stands in front of a full-length mirror, as she holds up a cocktail.* The woman was thinking, "I wish I didn't love to eat so much," and said, "Here's Nutra-diet to you!"

12. *Acrobats* both thought and said, "This is a tough act to follow."

13. *A bottle of pills held in a woman's hand* received no comment.

Comments. The disregard of limitations may have demonstrated either Kim's oppositional attitude toward the authority and/or a lack of self control. The procedural process plus the MPC appearance is an example of "acting-out art." It is often analogous to the way the client generally functions.

The photographs of the *obese women* who hate the way they look were probably conscious choices to depict her problem. The *fat beer-drinking man* also demonstrated Kim's compulsion to "fill" herself up, while the image of the *woman with the slim-fast cocktail* plus the *hand with pills* seemed to be a cue to Kim'a methods for keeping her figure.

Third Task

The third task was: *Pick out four, five, or six pictures of people and/or miscellaneous items that stand for something GOOD and something BAD. Paste them down and write or tell what the pictures mean.*

Kim's style remained consistent when she hastily chose an excessive number of photos. Large amounts of glue were sloppily applied. As before, the pictorial placement filled the entire page with overlapped images that went beyond the paper boundaries.

The GOOD illustrations (Figure 6C) included:

1-5. *Females and food*: one picture of a *woman whose is hiding her figure behind a towel* meant, "When I eat, I feel sooo good!"

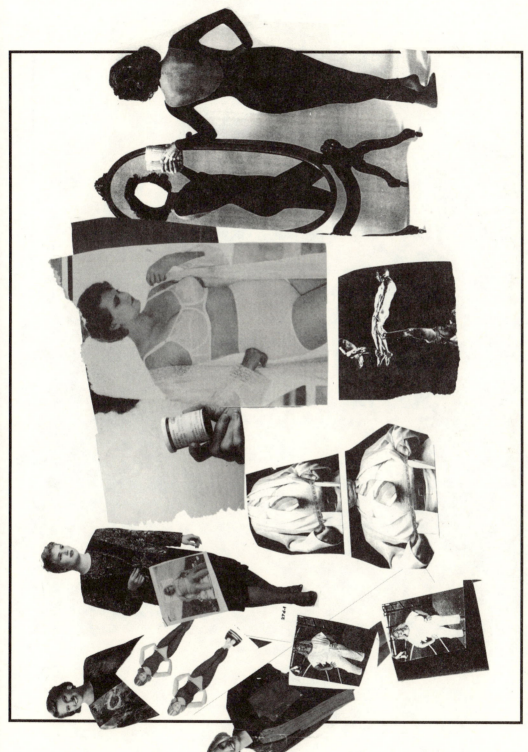

FIGURE 6B

FIGURE 6C

Because Kim had used up the entire page, she requested a second piece of paper for the BAD parts of her life.

The BAD examples (Figure 6D) included:

1. *Three identical women,* was a metaphor for, "being fat enough for three people."
2. A *houseworker with her forefinger to her mouth* identified, "keeping secrets."
3. The *woman out in nature with a gun tied to her back* symbolized, "hunting down animals."
4. The *grocery cart filled with food* represented, "buying too much food."

Comments. Kim's process remained consistent with an individual who lacks the control to stay within set limits. This is exemplified through her excessive pictorial selection, slipshod method of pasting, and going beyond the parameters of the page. Overall, the client seemed unable to set out a designated plan and tended to "wing it."

The GOOD items signified Kim's desire for food, whereas the BAD things alluded to her eating habits and her bulimic secret. The *animal hunt* free association could be related to the primitive part of herself, one that functions on primary process and fragments the superego for self discipline.

The photograph of a *grocery shopping cart* seemed to hold more information than merely buying food, since the market aisle shelves held drugs and sundry items. It might have alluded to her use of laxatives and diet pills for weight loss.

Fourth Task

The fourth task was: *Pick out only ONE picture of a person and paste it onto the page. Write or tell what you imagine is HAPPENING to that person.*

Kim was pleased to discover a picture of *one woman with twelve mouths being fed*. She pasted it down with a great deal of glue. With flourish, she surrounded it with four photographs of *food*. Once again the pictures overlapped and hung off the page. She said it referred to "overeating" (Figure 6E).

Kim was asked: *Will the situation change?* When she responded affirmatively, she was instructed to *pick out a picture and/or tell how it will come about*.

Her solution through an MPC (Figure 6F) included:

1. *A doctor with a patient on an x-ray table* with the answer, "liposuction."

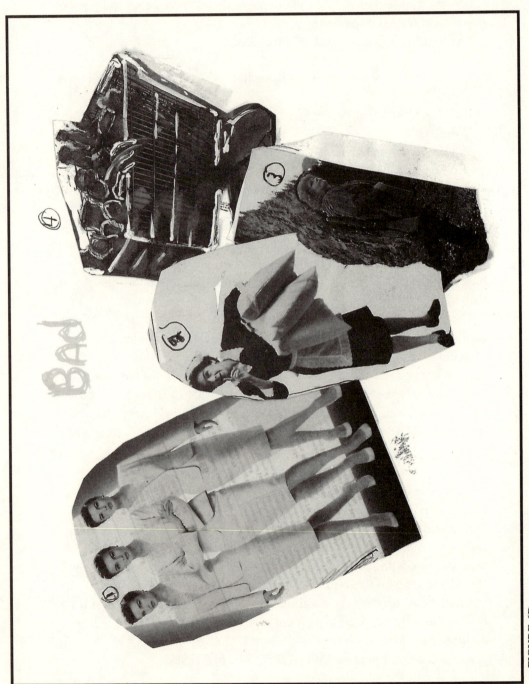

FIGURE 6D

FIGURE 6E

FIGURE 6F

2. *A woman in a market going through the drugstore section* with the reference, "One could take laxatives."
3. *A blonde woman* symbolized, "getting therapy."

Comments. Kim's impulsiveness was demonstrated, again, when she picked out three pictures instead of one as directed. Her obesity solutions embodied a "quick fix." The inclusion of "getting therapy" seemed an attempt to impress the therapist or perhaps she was sincere about making a commitment to therapy.

The treatment recommendation included both an insight orientation and a behavior modification approach.

Hispanic 30-Year-Old Male: Grief and Pre-Mourning

Roberto Colindo was unmarried. He was the youngest member of the family and the only one who lived in the United States with his mother. His six siblings lived in Central America. The client's father had died of a heart attack the previous year. His mother, in the last stage of terminal cancer, was in critical condition.

One month previously, Roberto under duress had placed his mother in a hospice care unit. He was in tremendous anguish and felt guilty about the move. The client could not believe that his mother would soon be dead. He still questioned the doctors' prognosis and had not dared to say good-bye to his mother. Therapy was given to him as a part of the hospice program.

First Task

The first task was: *Look through the box of miscellaneous items and pick out pictures that catch your attention. Paste them onto the paper. Next, write on the page or tell anything that comes to mind about each picture.*

Roberto was impatient to get this part of the interview over. Although the pictorial choices were made quickly, he took time to cut down several images to fit them on the page. The pasting and placement were done efficiently. Free associations were made swiftly to speed up the assessment.

The MPC (Figure 7A) included:

1. *The blonde woman at a computer* (with some likeness to this author) was accompanied by, "This lady is figuring something out."
2. A *penny* elicited the comment, "A penny doesn't do anything."
3. The *telephone* was a reference to, "waiting for a bad news call."

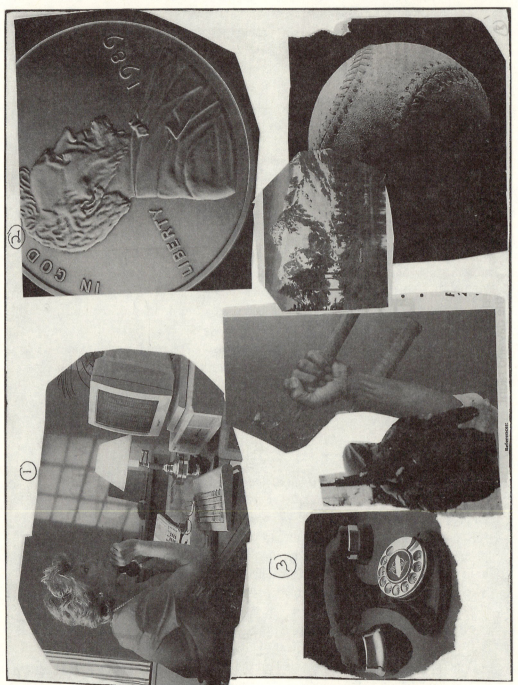

FIGURE 7A

4. *A soldier marching with a gun* meant, "He's off to kill for freedom."
5. *The hand holding a hammer* was identified with, "He's a carpenter like me."
6. *The snow-capped mountains* represented, "A pretty scary situation to be in."
7. *A baseball* brought the comment, "I'm very good at the game."

Comments. Several guesses seemed plausible. The *blonde woman* who resembled the therapist appeared to be a positive transference image. The *phone call* with bad news was realistically the hospital call that Roberto was awaiting. The *soldier* "off to kill" symbolized his anger over his mother's suffering and his forthcoming loss. Lastly, the *snow-capped mountain* that was "pretty scary" seemed to parallel his own fear of being left out in the cold, without any family to turn to.

Second Task

The second task was: *Pick out four, five or six pictures from the people box and paste them down on the paper. Next, write or tell what each person is THINKING and what he or she is SAYING.*

The MPC (Figure 7B) included:

1. *A Hispanic man playing a guitar* was both thinking and saying, "I'll sing a sad song."
2. *A doctor wearing a mask* was thinking, "It's bad there is no hope," and said, "We're sorry that we can't help you."
3. *A serious looking Hispanic boy* was thinking, "I'll be all alone," yet he pronounced, "I'm tough, leave me alone."
4. *A smiling Hispanic boy* was thinking, "I'm happy," and exclaimed, "I'm going fishing."
5. *The Hispanic soldier shooting a gun* was thinking, "They are bad, I'm going to kill them," and said, "I'm going to kill you."

Comments. Roberto personalized the task when he used only Hispanic people in his collage. The thoughts and statements were congruent, except for the boy who was sadly thinking about being left alone, but said he did not want to be bothered. This statement was probably meant for the therapist, who might be intrusive.

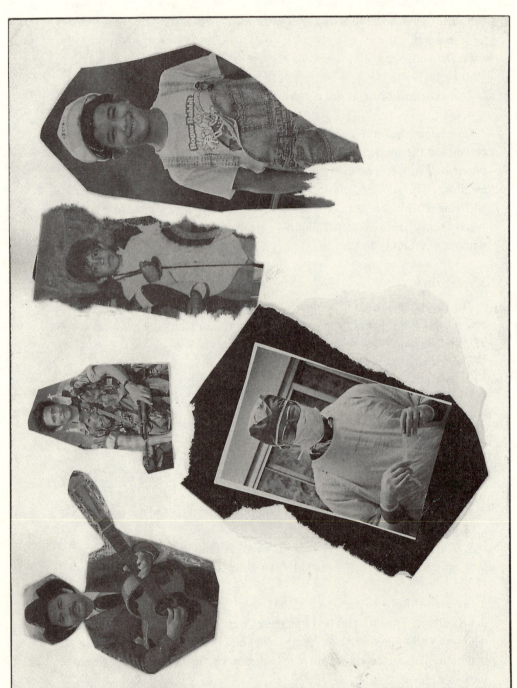

FIGURE 7B

Third Task

The third task was: *Pick out four, five, or six pictures of people and/or miscellaneous items that stand for something GOOD and something BAD. Paste them down and write or tell what the pictures mean.*

The GOOD and BAD representations were placed onto one page (Figure 7C). The GOOD symbols included:

1. *A Caucasian woman in a bathing suit*, which meant, "Sex is good."
2. The *man driving a red sports car* represented, "Heavy wheels is good."
3. The *man in underwear* stood for, "I'm strong and healthy."
4. *Food* was simply, "A good meal is good."
5. *Man on a treadmill* symbolized, "Exercise is good."
6. *Beer* meant, "Beer is good."

The BAD representations included:

1. *A gasoline tank* was the metaphor, "running out of gas is bad."
2. *A man being tied up by a guerrilla soldier* symbolized, "Being tied up and helpless is bad."

Comments. The excessive number of GOOD illustrations pointed out Roberto's need to remember his "soothing" involvements. The BAD picture of the *tank running out of gas* was a simile for Roberto's mother, whose life was almost at the end of its road. The *captive* who was rendered helpless paralleled his own impotence around his mother's condition.

Fourth Task

The fourth task was: *Pick out only ONE picture of a person, and paste it onto the page. Write or tell what you imagine is HAPPENING to that person.*

Without hesitation, Roberto picked the picture of *a doctor at a patient's bedside* (Figure 7D). He sadly commented, "The doctor can't help the person who is dying." When asked, *Will the situation change?* He replied, "Yeah." He was then instructed to *find a picture or tell how it will come about.*

Roberto was shocked to find a picture of a *priest praying over a Hispanic woman, while a grieving young Hispanic male soldier is holding her hand.* Taken off guard, Roberto began to sob as he said, "I'd better call in the priest for my mother."

Comments. The MPC helped Roberto to confront his mother's impending death. He realized that he could no longer delay his religious duty. The next day he activated himself to call in the priest for his mother's last rites.

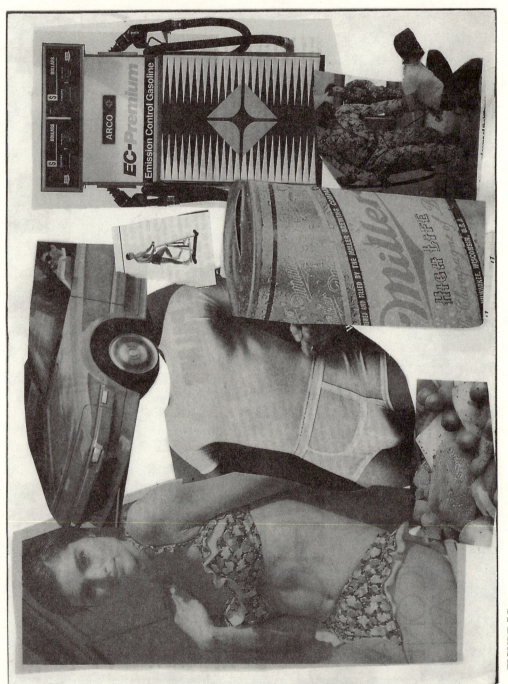

FIGURE 7C

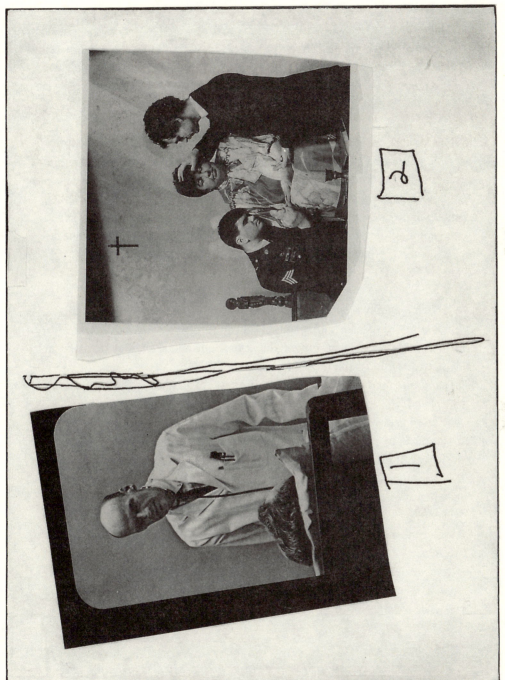

FIGURE 7D

Hispanic 44-Year-Old Male: Post-Traumatic Stress Disorder

Juan was married and had four children. He reported recurring nightmares and suffered from anxiety. He lost 20 pounds in several months and was making mistakes on his carpentry job.

First Task

The first task was: *Look through the box of miscellaneous items and pick out pictures that catch your attention. Paste them onto the paper. Next, write on the page or tell anything that comes to mind about each picture.*

Juan was nervous when he fumbled through the pictures, but he seemed intent upon picking out certain images. With shaky hands he applied glue and pasted some of the photos down in overlapped positions in order to squeeze them all onto the page. His free associations came readily.

The MPC (Figure 8A) included:

1. *A hand holding a micrometer with drill bits next to it* was used to explain, "I've got to measure things right on my job."
2. *The large number of human skulls* brought about tears as he said, "it stands for all of the men that I saw die in Nam."
3. *A missile being shot off* was identified as, "The missiles kill everything around."
4. *The cloth covering an unknown object* conjured up the statement, "When it comes to war, I just want to hide away."
5. *Statue of Liberty* stood for, "freedom when there is no more war."
6. *Mouse headed for the cheese in a rattrap* symbolized, "We never know when we'll come across the next trap where we could get killed."

Comments. Juan's pictorial and verbal statements were a testimony to his sufferings as a soldier in Vietnam. The overseas war that was going on at the time was shown on television and reminded him of his own war experiences. It was obvious that the client was suffering from Post-Traumatic Stress Disorder.

Second Task

The second task was: *Pick out four, five, or six pictures from the people box and paste them onto the paper. Next, write or tell what each person is THINKING and what he or she is SAYING.*

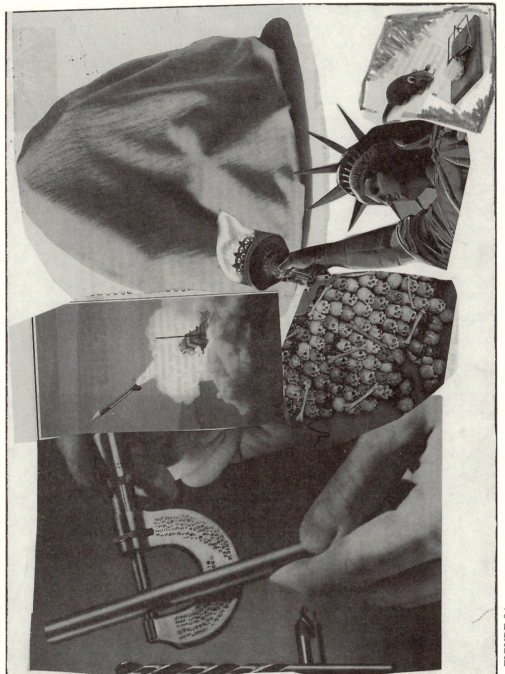

FIGURE 8A

Juan's photographic choices were all in black and white, even though the vast majority available were in color.

The MPC (Figure 8B) included:

1. *The Hispanic man playing tennis* was thinking, "I'm too old for this game," yet he said, "Hit a hard ball."
2. *A young Hispanic male holding a machine gun* was thinking, "I'm too young to die," but bravely announced, "Come on and try to get us. Me and my buddies are going to finish you off."
3. *A Hispanic boy reading a book* was thinking, "I hate to study," and said, "Okay I'm going to college."
4. *The female Hispanic woman singer* was thinking, "I feel sexy" while she sang, "Besame Mucho."
5. *The Mexican wrestling champion* thought, "Boy, I've taken a beating, I hurt all over," as he uttered, "Thank you."

Comments. The disparities appear in the male figures. These seemed in keeping with the "macho" image, where men hide their vulnerable thoughts and feelings.

Third Task

The third task was: *Pick out four, five, or six pictures of people and/or miscellaneous items that stand for something GOOD and something BAD. Paste them down and write or tell what the pictures mean.*

Juan was so involved with looking out for GOOD things that he seemed to forget the selection limitation. He did not write the meanings since the statements were clear without any words (Figure 8C).

The GOOD representations included:

1. *A milkshake.*
2. *A Madonna statue.*
3. *Hispanic prizefighter.*
4. *Hispanic baseball player.*
5. *Hispanic boy playing a musical instrument.*
6. *Hispanic woman in a bathtub.*
7. *Head of an attractive Hispanic woman.*

The BAD representations on the right side included:

1. *Soldiers with guns.*

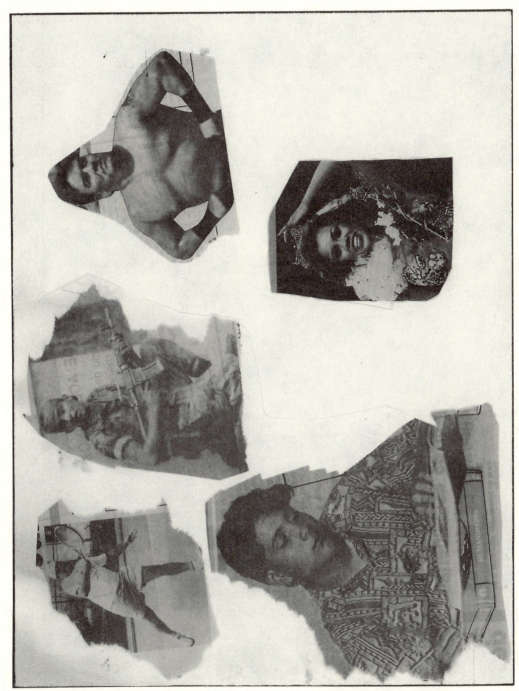

FIGURE 8B

FIGURE 8C

2. *Hispanic surgeons performing an operation.*
3. *Man and woman praying in a graveyard.*

Comments. The large number of GOOD metaphors indicated that Juan was in touch with the things that could bring him enjoyment. BAD representations were consistent with the recurring memories of his wartime ordeal.

Fourth Task

The fourth task was: *Pick out only ONE picture of a person, then paste it onto the page. Write or tell what you imagine is HAPPENING to that person.*

Juan chose the picture of Salvadoran soldiers. He claimed that the picture spoke for itself. He was asked if the *situation will change.* When he indicated that it would, he was instructed to find a picture or tell how it would come about.

Juan's reply was through a picture of a *Hispanic mother and children walking down a hillside* (Figure 8D). He explained that the solution would be an escape to the United States.

Comments. Juan's solution choice related to his early childhood, when he and his parents fled El Salvador. The current war overseas rekindled past traumas of fear, death, and loss.

The response to the situational change was "escape." Just as the photograph showed the people fleeing from their problems, Juan, too, wished to flee from his own war guilt and memories.

Asian-American 45-Year-Old Male: Suicidal Ideation

David sought therapy because of his depressed state. His wife had recently asked for a divorce because she was in love with another man. The client was staggered by this event. He had assumed that his spouse was as satisfied with their marriage as he was.

David reported a loss of appetite and sleep difficulties. He blamed these problems on his ruminations about "trying to figure out where did I go wrong with my marriage." He was having a hard time waking up and going to work. Too embarrassed to face friends shared with his wife, he withdrew socially.

First Task

Instructions for the first task were: *Look through the box of miscellaneous items and pick out pictures that catch your attention. Paste them onto the*

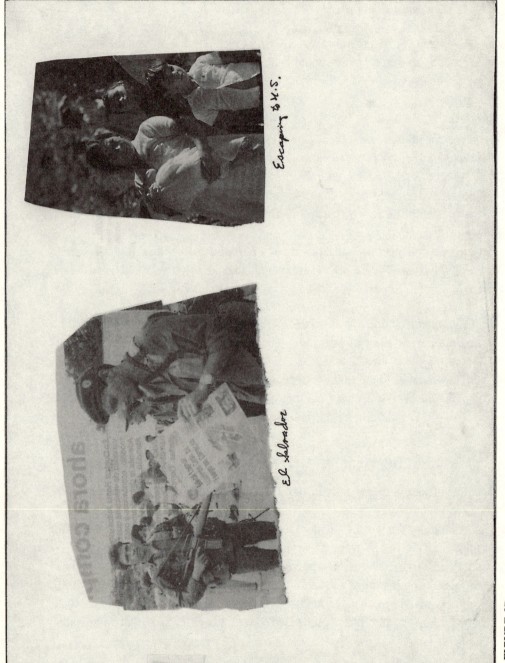

Escaping to U.S.

El salvador

FIGURE 8D

paper. Next, write on the page or tell anything that comes to mind about each picture.

David was lethargic in his approach. He selected only two images. Both of them were black and white although the majority of photographs were in color. His pasting was slow but neat, and the pictures were placed evenly and far apart.

The MPC (Figure 9A) included:

1. *A polluted city* brought the comment, "Not enough attention is paid to the ecology. The planet was in bad shape."
2. *A looped rope that formed a noose* caused David to hesitate before he made any comment. He failed to express the meaning and wrote, "It's just a rope."

Comments. It appeared that David might be suicidal. Pollution, the neglect of the ecology, and the planet being "in bad shape" appeared to represent his own psychological state. This notion was strengthened by the image of a "noose." This symbol is sometimes used by persons with suicidal ideation. The client either blocked or chose not to reveal the meaning of the rope. Either way, an alert for additional suicidal clues was set in motion.

Second Task

The second task was: *Pick out four, five, or six pictures from the people box and paste them onto the paper. Next, write or tell what each person is THINKING and what he or she is SAYING.*

David picked out the minimum number of four pictures. Once again, they were all in black and white. Languid in his approach, he was neat in his pasting and placement.

The MPC (Figure 9B) contained:

1. *A Caucasian man in pain holding the sides of his head* was thinking, "I can't stand this any longer," yet he merely said, "Hello."
2. *A man at a computer* was thinking, "I can't figure this out," but he said, "No problem, I'm taking care of everything."
3. *A Japanese woman,* who David mentioned resembled his wife, was thinking, "I'm going to do my own thing," and said, "I'm going my way."
4. *A Caucasian smiling man* was thinking, "It's no use," but in contrast said, "I'm fine."

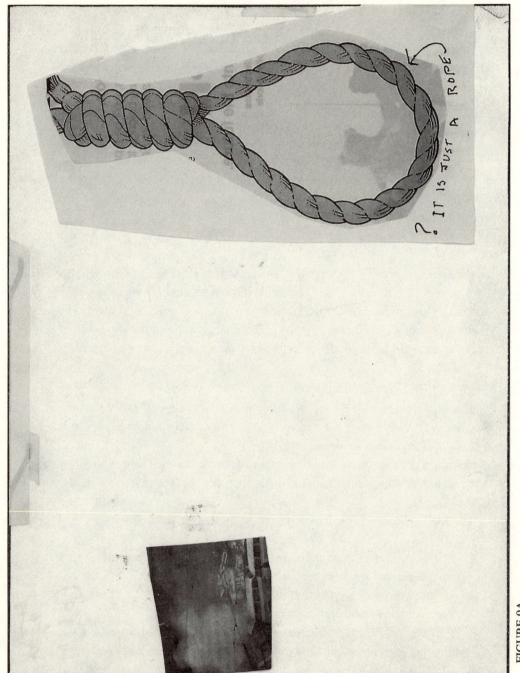

FIGURE 9A

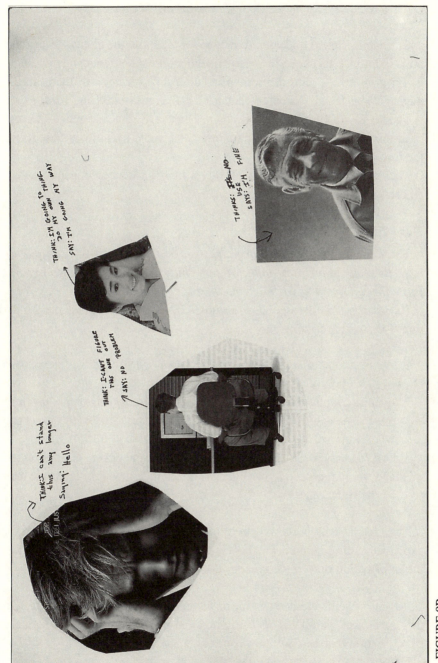

Although there were many pictures of Japanese men in the people box, David's male selections were all Caucasians.

Comments. Suicidal ideation continued throughout the client's free associations. The incongruence between thoughts and statements showed David's inclination toward secrecy, perhaps a cultural factor due to "saving face." It might also be denial as a defense against his feelings of loss and abandonment.

The MPC expressed David's despair. The use of Caucasian men was a way of distancing himself from his pain or an attempt to mask his problems from the therapist.

The only thoughts and statements that were congruent belonged to his wife, whose message was clear.

Third Task

The third task was: *Pick out four, five, or six pictures of people and/or miscellaneous items that stand for something GOOD and something BAD. Paste them down and write or tell what the pictures mean.*

David immediately responded (Figure 9C). He decided to pick out the BAD things first. These included:

1. *A punctured fire extinguisher with the fluid pouring out* was accompanied by, "It's no use, it won't put out the fire."
2. *A Caucasian homeless family with the father carrying a sign asking for a job so he can feed his family* was chosen because, "I saw this exact scene when I got off the freeway."
3. The *freeway traffic jam* meant, "That drives me crazy, just sitting there and waiting, especially when I can't do anything about it. I'm at the mercy of the situation."

The GOOD was portrayed by pictures of *binoculars* and a *bird.* David explained, "Birdwatching is a hobby that I've had for years, I've put a lot of the information onto my computer about birds."

Comments. David avoided making any overt references to his problems. Only the "traffic jam" paralleled his frustration and anger about being at the "mercy" of a situation that he could not control.

However, on a covert level, the "fire extinguisher" seemed a symbol for his impotence around the issue of divorce. It was also plausible that it referred to his rage, the internal fire, which he was unable to distinguish.

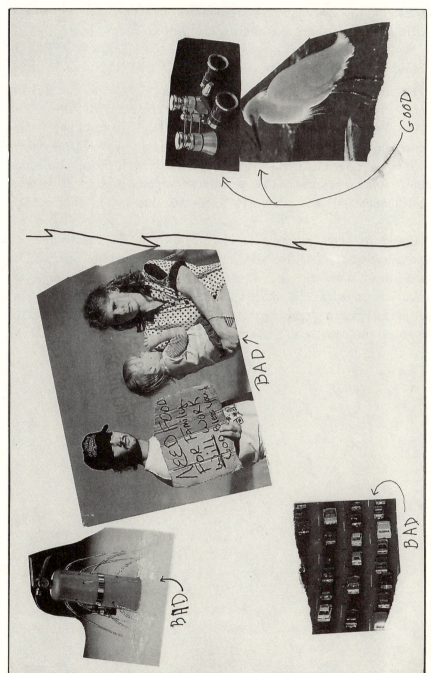

GOOD

BAD

BAD

BAD

FIGURE 9C

The "homeless man" who needed to "feed his family" was analogous to his own feelings of abandonment and emotional starvation.

The GOOD representation showed his involvement in a hobby.

Fourth Task

The fourth task was: *Pick out only ONE picture of a person, then paste it onto the page. Write or tell what you imagine is HAPPENING to that person.*

David spent little time on this task. He immediately spotted a photo of *coal miners* and declared, "A coal miner died." When he was asked *if the situation will change*, he replied, "Yes." He was then instructed to *pick a picture or tell how it would come about*. The response was a photograph of a *cemetery* to show that the only alternative was "to get the miner buried" (Figure 9D).

Comments. David's despair was blatantly evident. Suicidal ideation was a strong possibility. Since the MPC exhibited his reticence to voice what was on his mind, it was necessary to confront the issue of suicide straight on.

David acknowledged a plan to kill himself. He would take pills in his possession and place a plastic bag over his head. David agreed to hospitalization and was relieved to be in a safe place where he could not kill himself.

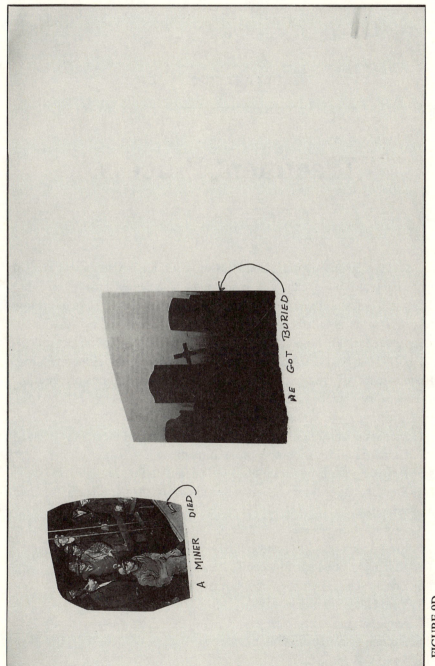

FIGURE 9D

CHAPTER 5

Treatment Process

The MPC can be an important and innovative aid for any treatment goal. It may be integrated into the therapy at any point. The therapist may wish to use it in several ways: a) one or more times in a single session; b) one or more times in a series of sessions; c) once at the beginning of every session. Examples of each are demonstrated in the treatment illustrations that follow.

The MPC can be utilized for any goal, short or long term. A therapist may introduce it for any reason, at any time, since the possiblities are endless.

Case history vignettes include the following MPC objectives:

1. Managing cultural differences between client and therapist.
2. Easing minority group people into treatment.
3. Providing a means for cultural self-identification.
4. Employing a tool for understanding clients from their cultural frame of reference.
5. Concretizing issues.
6. Providing a quasi substitute for language with the resistant client.
7. Serving as an agent for recall.
8. Encouraging fantasies through pictorial imagery.
9. Ventilating emotions.
10. Sublimating material.
11. Serving as a transitional object.
12. Rehearsal for action.
13. Transference state.

14. Expressing emotions.
15. Gaining awareness.
16. Unconscious means for revealing information.
17. Suicidal ideation clues.
18. Making conscious declarations.
19. Indicators for gender identity confusion.
20. A benign testing ground for the client to check out therapist's reactions.
21. Loosening of defenses to reveal drug abuse.
22. Concretizing strengths and weaknesses.
23. Revealing secrets.
24. Displaying illusions or delusions.
25. Unmasking of humor as a defense mechanism.
26. Exploring sexual issues.
27. Examining cause and effect.
28. Positive life review.
29. Exploring family dynamics.

The MPC orientation should coincide with the issues that are being dealt with. The task instructions may be open and *direct* (using the *first person*), or *indirect through a metaphor* that runs on a parallel path (using the *third person*). Another option is a *free choice* where general free associations take place.

For instance, in a case where a Caucasian couple had recently divorced, the physical custody of the children was divided between the mother and father. The seven-year-old boy, Tom (the designated acting-out client), lived with his father; his two-year-old sister stayed with her mother. When the boy was seen alone, there were two alternative instructions for dealing with the emotions around the divorce, either through *direct* instructions *(pick out pictures that show how you feel about each person in your family)* or through the *indirect* approach *(pick out pictures of animals and make up an animal family story)*.

Tom's guilt over his divided loyalties would have made the direct technique too threatening. Therefore, the metaphor technique was used. His MPC (Figure 10A) held pictures of *two Dalmations, one large, the other small, plus a large pig kissing a piglet.* When told to give voices to the animals, Tom identified the dogs as a father and son and the pigs as a mother and her baby. He dealt with alliances and expressed his anger toward his mother, ambivalence about his sister, and positive feelings for his father. In this way, Tom managed to ventilate his emotions safely and to sublimate.

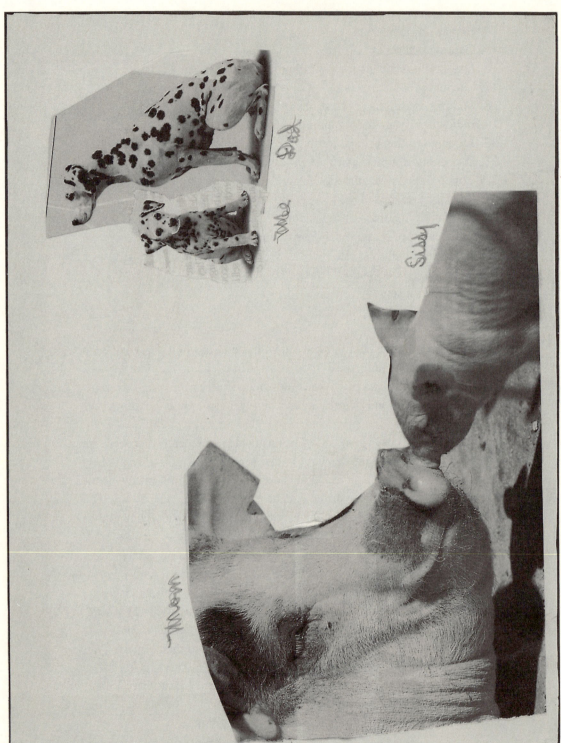

FIGURE 10A

Both methods are also available with adolescents and adults. For example, Linda, an Asian young adult, believed she had to cover up her feelings because, "That pleases everyone." It was essential that the client portray the emotional side of herself to the therapist. An indirect approach was inappropriate and the direct method was used. Linda was directed: *Select two pictures, one that shows the FACE you SHOW to the WORLD and another that shows how you FEEL on the INSIDE.* Linda's "outside picture" was of a HAPPY Asian woman (Figure 11A). While the "inside photo" revealed a woman with a ZIPPERED MOUTH as FEAR and DEPRESSION covered her face (Figure 11B).

Another time, when Linda had trouble expressing her anger in any open way, the indirect approach was used. She was told: *make THREE collages that show some people's feelings of: PLEASURE, FRUSTRATION, and ANGER.*

The first MPC about PLEASURE (Figure 11C) contained *an Asian girl with a slight smile on her face; an Asian man (who looks only possibly frustrated); and an Asian man (who, to the therapist, looks more concerned than angry).*

To give these emotions more distance, the art therapist gave these instructions next: *Pick out pictures of animals that show different emotions.* Linda found a large range of selections and had to use several pieces of paper that she had to glue together. Her collage included: *several dogs* who felt "happy," "sad," "excited," "satisfied"; a *monkey* that was "playfully gay"; a *wolf* that was "enraged"; a *bear* that experienced "pleasure"; and a *butterfly* that felt "free" (Figure 11D).

MPC TREATMENT ILLUSTRATIONS

The case-history examples that follow encompass material from clients who are Asian, Black, Caucasian, and Hispanic. These illustrations can be adapted to people from other cultures as well, providing the appropriate *people images* are at their disposal.

The vignettes in this chapter include the reasons for the utilization of the MPC with descriptions of its application. They demonstrate how the collage mode is used during a single session and in a number of consecutive sessions.

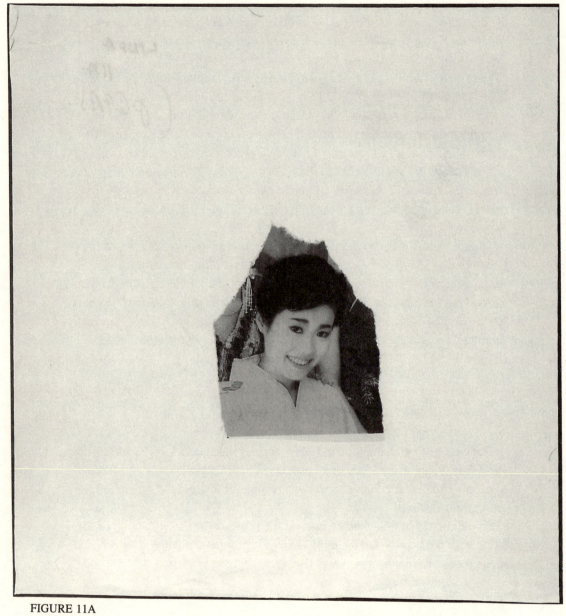

FIGURE 11A

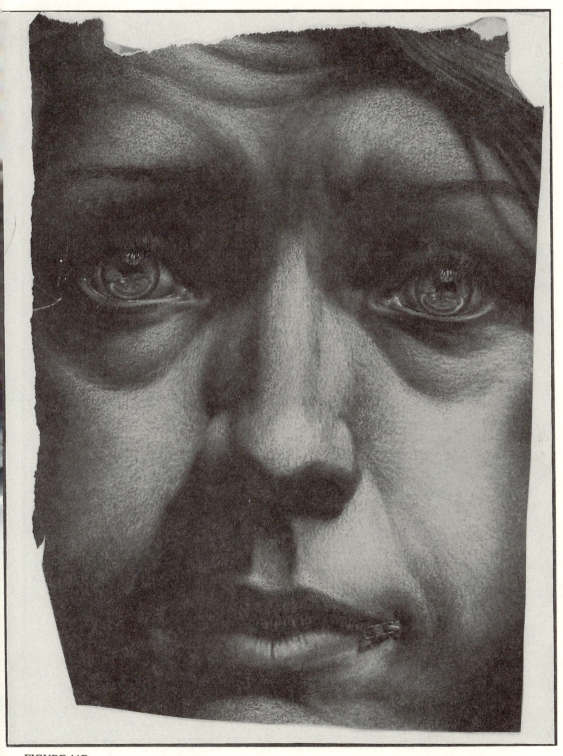

FIGURE 11B

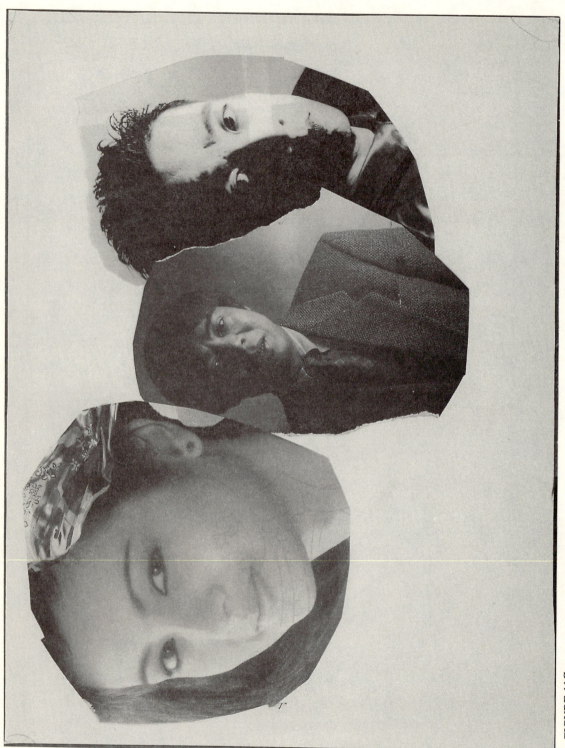

FIGURE 11C

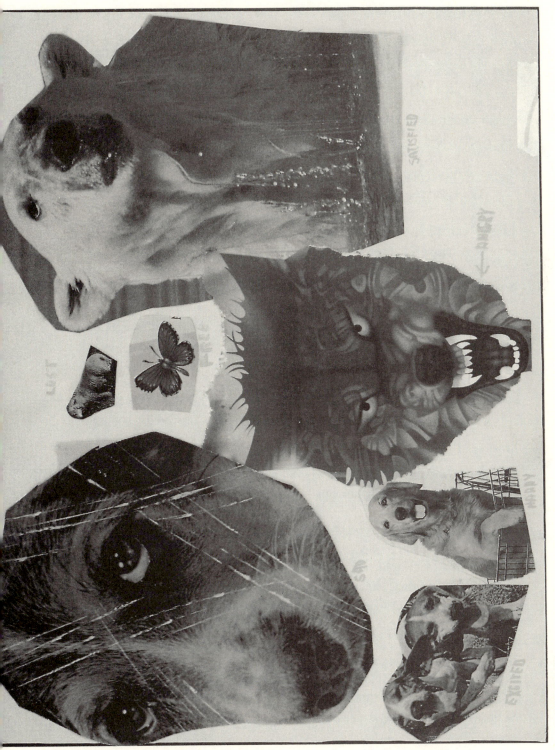

FIGURE 11D

Black Parent of a Four-Year-Old Child: The Primal Scene

Albertha Cole, a four-year-old child, was fearful of going to sleep and had recently become reluctant to leave her mother's side. Her parents reported that six months previously their daughter had been traumatized by an earthquake. Nevertheless, Albertha had slept well until a month ago.

When Mrs. Cole was seen alone, she was instructed: *Look over the magazine pictures and pick out any that might lead to clues for Albertha's behavior.* The MPC (Figure 12A) contained:

1. *A night scene with someone looking outside the home* represented Albertha's fear of sleeping.
2. *A destroyed house* recalled the memory, "The last earthquake scared me and Albertha. We were home alone because my husband had left for work early that day."
3. The *bee* reminded her that Albertha had been "stung by a bee." When questioned about the date of this event, she remembered that it was a year ago and ruled out this clue.
4. *A pointing finger* characterized, "the nursery school teacher who was provoked because my child had begun to wet her pants." When asked how long ago this had taken place, Mrs. Cole answered, "about three weeks ago."

Although Mrs. Cole believed this picture was the answer, she was encouraged to continue looking through the photos just in case other memories might be evoked.

She was astonished to find a picture that gave the answer. It was of a *crying child opening her parents' bedroom door while they were in bed* (Figure 12B). Until Mrs. Cole sighted this photograph, she had forgotten that the previous month an identical situation had occurred. Albertha had walked into the bedroom to find her mother and father "making love." Mrs. Cole recalled that she was moaning and considered how this might have frightened Albertha.

Comments. In the following meeting, the parents were helped to approach the subject of the primal scene with Albertha. The child's concern that her father had harmed her mother was alleviated and shortly afterwards Albertha's presenting symptoms disappeared.

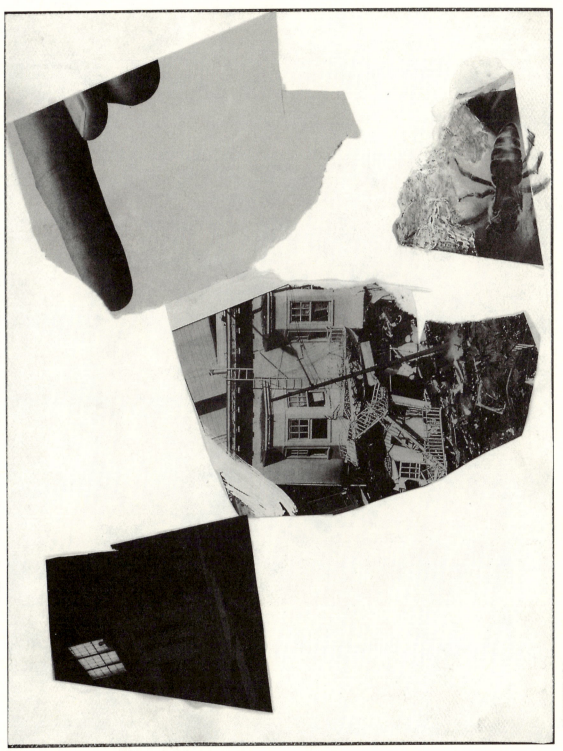

FIGURE 12A

FIGURE 12B

Caucasian 10-Year-Old Female: Withdrawn Behavior

Jane Root was seriously affected by her parent's divorce. She had always been her "daddy's favorite," while her brother, four years younger than herself, was "mommy's special child."

The teacher at school reported a change in Jane's attitude. She had become withdrawn and had trouble concentrating on her studies. The child often appeared lost in thought as she gazed out of the window. Peer relationships were also affected. Jane no longer made an effort to be an important part of group interactions.

Mrs. Root, too, was concerned about the altered behavior. Jane had previously been an active enthusiastic child, but was now listless and uninterested in anything except watching television.

When Jane began therapy, she was treated with the classical psychoanalytic approach. She remained silent, refused to be cooperative, and rarely responded to the therapist's overtures. When she did speak, she insisted, "I have NO PROBLEMS, the only problem I have is my parents' divorce." The child stubbornly added, "I want my mother and father to be married again so we'll all live together in our house like we use to!"

The only information that Jane offered was that her father had moved in with his girlfriend. With his new lifestyle, he had little time for her. Even though he telephoned regularly, Jane complained that she had not seen her father in over a month. In anger she declared, "He's always too busy for me."

Because Jane was uncooperative in therapy, the MPC was offered. Although reluctant, she did comply with the instructions. Jane's most positive response was to the directive: *Choose pictures of people, then write down or dictate what they are THINKING and what they are SAYING.* Consequently, this particular technique was used *each week,* with the added dimension of *story-telling about someone in the collage.*

Despite her involvement, Jane's passive-aggressive features were displayed by her deliberate slowness. Her delay tactics included: looking through every picture in the box, sometimes several times; a lackadaisical approach in decision-making; spending time to trim photos into unusual forms; considering which color construction paper to choose for the background; figuring out the placement of the pictures.

During this process, Jane frequently glanced sideways to catch a glimpse of the therapist's reactions to her slow-paced decision-making. The dictation was the only part of the procedure that was not belabored; it was expressed at a normal pace.

The child was allowed to be in control. As a result, only a single collage was created in each session.

First Session

In the first session, Jane chose the picture of a *Caucasian youth lying on a rock slab as he scoops up a drink of water.* He was thinking, "Please! Someone help me," but he said, "It sure is great to drink this water" (Figure 13A). The MPC inspired the following dictated story:

THE BOY LOST ON A ISLAND

ME AND MY FAMILY, WE WERE ALL ON A WEAK BOAT AND A STORM CAME AND WRECKED THE BOAT. MY FAMILY DIED. BUT I WAS FLOATED TO A DESERT ISLAND. AND WHEN I WOKE UP, I FELT SOMETHING ON MY BACK. I TURNED AROUND AND IT WAS A BABY BEAR. IT WAS REALLY CUTE. I PICKED IT UP. IT WAS REALLY SMALL.

I WAS REALLY THIRSTY SO I WENT OVER TO THE ROCKS AND I TOOK A NICE LONG DRINK AND I WASHED MY FACE. I LOOKED ABOVE THE ROCK AND I SAW A BOAT. I MADE A SIGNAL FIRE AND THEY CAME OVER AND RESCUED ME. I WAS LIVING WHERE CHILDREN ARE ADOPTED WITH MY CUDDLY BABY BEAR.

I FOUND A HOME AND I LIVED HAPPILY EVER AFTER WITH MY NEW MOTHER AND FATHER AND MY CUDDLY BEAR.

THE END
The writer of this story is JANE ROOT

Comments. When Jane was asked if she owned a "toy bear," she said her dad had given her one a long time ago. This transitional object brought comfort to her both in reality and in the story.

The tale goes on to relate that she and her family are on a "wrecked boat" where everyone except herself dies. In life, she had experienced the "wreck" and "death" of her family unit. Yet, in the story Jane replenishes herself and is rescued. This is the compensatory wish to have a family that is complete once again.

Second Session

In the second week, Jane chose the picture of a *woman hiding in a garbage*

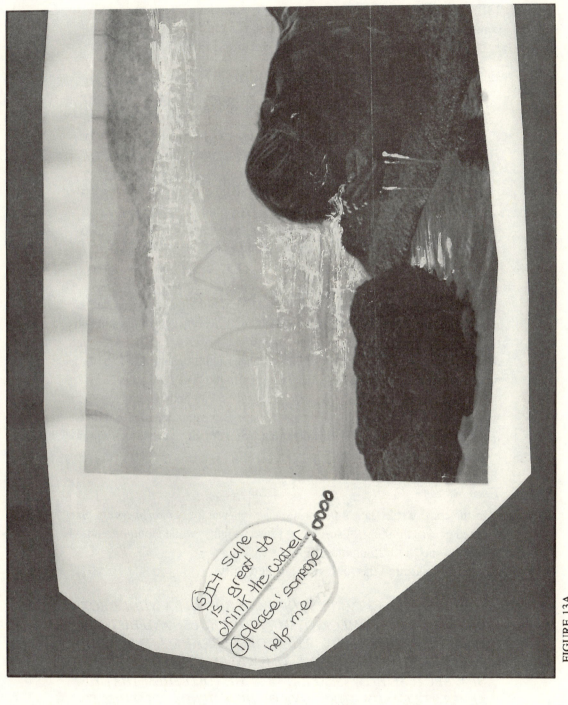

FIGURE 13A

can. Only the eyes, forehead, and cascading hair over the can are seen (Figure 13B). The child remarked that the woman was thinking, "I am so scared!" In contrast, she said, "Hey, Chicken, come over here."

The MPC inspired the following dictated story:

> *THIS IS A WOMAN WHO WAS WATCHING A SCARY MOVIE. SHE WAS SO SCARED SHE JUMPED INTO A GARBAGE CAN. SHE SLEPT OVERNIGHT IN THE TRASH CAN AND IN THE MORNING SOME PEOPLE TEASED HER BECAUSE SHE WAS SCARED AND SLEPT IN THE GARBAGE CAN. SHE ACTED BRAVE AND GOT OUT OF THE GARBAGE CAN AND CHASED THE PEOPLE AWAY. THEN THAT NIGHT SHE WAS BACK IN HER HOUSE AND WHEN SHE STEPPED INTO THE DOOR SHE WENT INTO THE TWILIGHT ZONE. BUT THEN SHE FIGURED OUT THE WHOLE THING WAS A DREAM AND THEN SHE LIVED HAPPILY EVER AFTER.*
>
> *The name of this story is THE SCARY DREAM by Jane Root*

Comments. The woman who is frightened by watching a scary movie may represent her mother, with whom she identifies. Bravery is one of the strengths that is revealed as she confronts the persons who teased her. Yet, Jane, who denies her present circumstances, experiences her life as unreal. This is analogous to the person in the story who enters the "twilight zone."

The child refuses to believe that her former life, with both parents together, will never return. Therefore, she ends the story by using denial as a defense mechanism and declares, "The whole thing was a dream and she lives happily ever after."

Third Session

In the third week, Jane's pictorial selection was of a *man jogging*. She claimed he was thinking, "I sure hope I lose weight," while aloud he said, "I told everyone I lost 25 pounds" (Figure 13C).

The MPC inspired the following dictated story:

> *HE WENT INTO A CANDY STORE AND BOUGHT A WHOLE BOX OF CANDY BARS. SOMEONE CAME TO HIS HOUSE AND HE TOLD THEM HE HATED CANDY. WHEN THEY LEFT HE ATE ALL THE CANDY BARS. WHEN HE WENT SOMEWHERE, EVERYONE TEASED HIM, BECAUSE HE WAS SO FAT, BUT HE TOLD THEM THAT HE NEVER ATE CANDY. THEN, ONE OF HIS FRIENDS TOLD HIM TO*

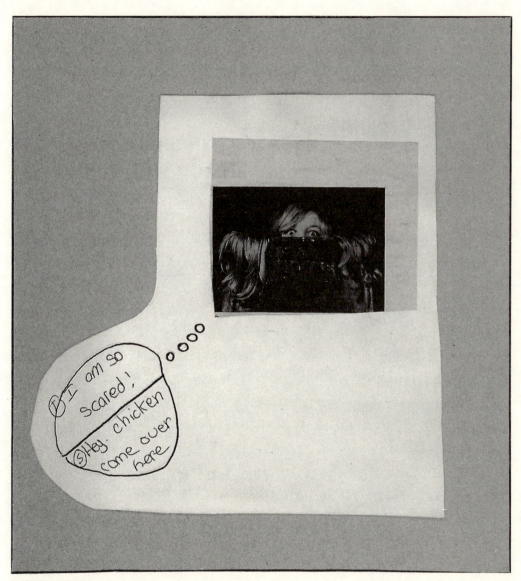

FIGURE 13B

FIGURE 13C

*GO TO EXERCISE CLASS AND TO START JOGGING BECAUSE THEY
KNEW HE WAS LYING. THEN HE STOPPED LYING AND STARTED
JOGGING AND IT WAS LIKE A MIRACLE BECAUSE HE GOT THIN
AND NEVER LIED AGAIN.*
The name of this story is THE LYING MAN by JANE ROOT

Comments. The story about the "lying man" was related to Jane's father,
whom she called a "liar" whenever he canceled their appointments. One of the
child's positive aspects was her ability to confront "the truth." As before, she
ends the tale with the compensatory wish that he will change.

Fourth Session

In the fourth week, Jane selected the *portrait of a Caucasian man with a
slight smile on his face who is wearing a sport jacket with a shirt and tie* (Figure
13D). The man was thinking, "I can't wait till I get home because it's my son's
birthday," and said, "My son's birthday is today, that's great." The next day
was actually Jane's brother's birthday.

The MPC inspired the following dictated story:

*THIS MAN HAS A WIFE AND TWO KIDS. A BOY SIX AND A GIRL
TWELVE. HE IS JUST SO HAPPY THAT HE GOES HOME FOR HIS
SON'S BIRTHDAY. HIS SON IS NOT THERE SO THEY PLAN THIS
SURPRISE PARTY AND THE KID GETS LOT OF PRESENTS.*
The name of this story is THE HAPPY SURPRISE by Jane Root

Comments. The "happy surprise" is Jane's wish that her father will show up
for her brother's birthday. Although the child will not state this directly, she
uses the stories to express her wishes.

Fifth–Eighth Sessions

In the fifth through the eighth sessions, Jane continued to take charge of the
meetings. She arranged the collage boxes and other materials on her own, then
proceeded to make up the same "thinking and saying tasks" and accompanied
them with her stories. These creations did not disclose any new material.
Regardless, since the child was comfortable with this form of expression, it
was resumed in each session. At that point in therapy, it was obvious that Jane
knew that her art and stories were of a personal nature.

FIGURE 13D

In the eighth session, Jane carefully created the following MPC (Figure 13E):

1. *A car-testing female dummy with the ears taped up* was not thinking or saying anything because, "It's only a dummy, they can't hear or talk."
2. *A blonde woman (whose hair and age were similar to the therapist's).* Much care was taken with trimming around this image. Jane looked directly at the therapist and said, "This lady thinks that children are nice." She says, "That's good."
3. A *smiling girl* thinks, "I'm smiling because I'm feeling better," and says, "I was sick for a long time with a secret disease, but now it's disappearing."

Jane said she did not want to make up a story about this MPC. On her own initiative, she created another collage (Figure 13F). When she found the photograph of a *man, two children, and a young woman, all wearing baseball caps and looking happy,* she tore away the image of the woman. Jane adamantly declared, "I'm not going to make up a story, 'cause there's nothing to say. Only they enjoyed themselves at the ball game with their father."

Comments. Apparently the torn-away female figure was a metaphor for her father's girlfriend. The dummy is analogous to her complaints about her father, whereas the blonde woman was an obvious transference statement. The child whose disease was disappearing hinted at her own improvement.

Ninth Session

When a therapeutic alliance had been formed, the MPC topics shifted to feelings. For Jane to ventilate her anger toward her father in a safe environment, she was instructed: *Make a collage that shows your ANGRY and GOOD feelings or memories about your dad.*

Jane, now familiar with the photos, had particular ones in mind.

The ANGRY MEMORIES (Figure 13G) included:

1. *A Caucasian man with the eyes missing* was identified as, "My dad doesn't see me enough."
2. *The portrait of a Caucasian man with his mouth taped up* meant, "He hardly ever talks to my face, it's on the phone."
3. *A smiling Caucasian man whose ears are cut off* symbolized her father's unwillingness to be available.

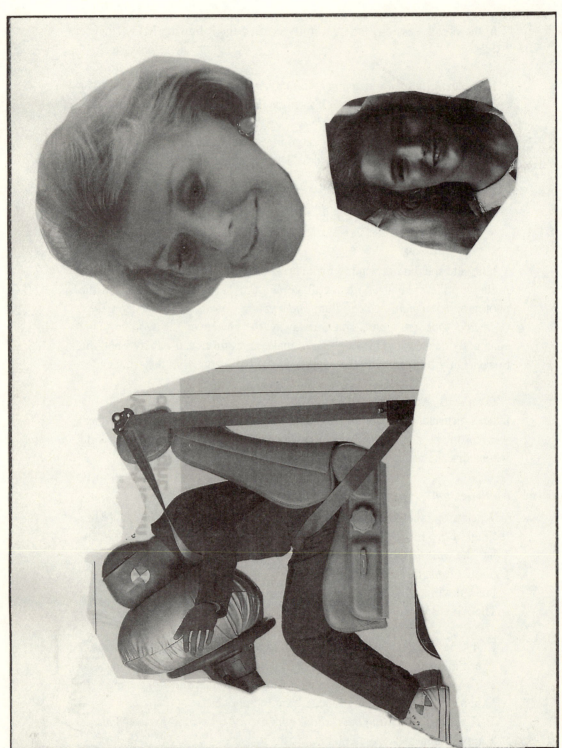

FIGURE 13E

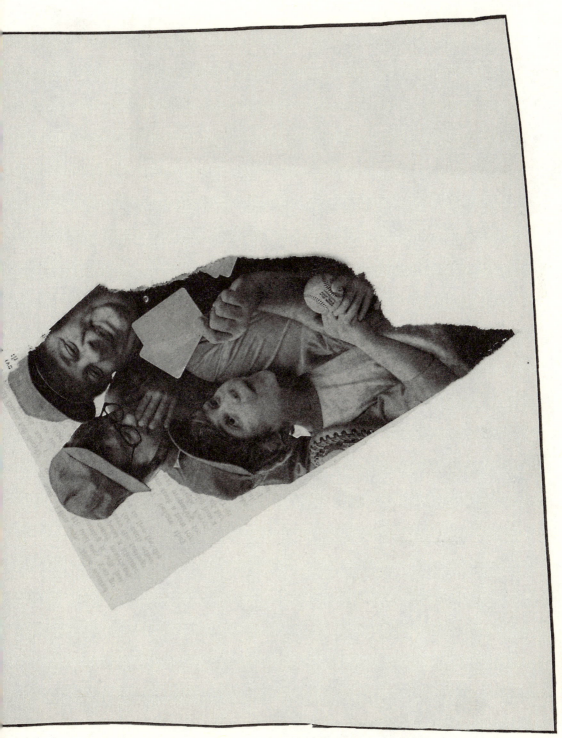

FIGURE 13F

FIGURE 13G

4. *A Caucasian man standing in a can, calling on a cordless phone,* illustrated, "When my dad calls me up it always sounds like he is far away. I think he calls from his car or his patio."
5. *The fearful-looking Caucasian woman* stood for, "My mommy worries about not having enough money."
6. *A Caucasian child with filled cheeks and a mouth shut tight* demonstrated, "That's how I feel sometimes, like vomiting, but I hold it in."

The one picture that Jane pondered over, yet failed to use was of a *man running with a large truck close behind him* (Figure 13H).

When the GOOD MEMORIES were considered, none came to mind. Jane was encouraged to keep looking through the images. Although resistant, she probably gave in to please the therapist.

The MPC (Figure 13I) included:

1. *A man and child fishing,* Jane said, did not need an explanation.
2. *A happy woman and man* was also self evident.
3. *The silhouette of a man with a child on his knees* meant, "My dad used to play with me."
4. *An older man ready to kiss a little girl* stood for, "He used to give me smoochie kisses."

The collage reminded Jane of her losses. As the meeting was nearing the end, it was necessary to bring some closure to the session. Consequently, she was told; *Make a collage with only two pictures that stand for something you wish you could say to your dad.*

The MPC (figure not shown) included:

1. A *car* (the color of her father's) meant, "Come and get me so we can go out and have fun."
2. *Food* represented her wish, "Come get me, Daddy, we'll go in the car and go out for a hamburger and french fries, and we'll talk about things."

Jane was asked if she had ever been explicit in relating her needs to her father. She was unable to recall if she had ever confronted him directly.

Comments. The session was influential. That week Jane talked to her father and told him exactly what she had role-played in the collage. To her surprise, he paid attention and picked her up in his car and went out to eat. She found that being clear and direct brought results. On other occasions, Jane also used the collage as a rehearsal vehicle.

FIGURE 13H

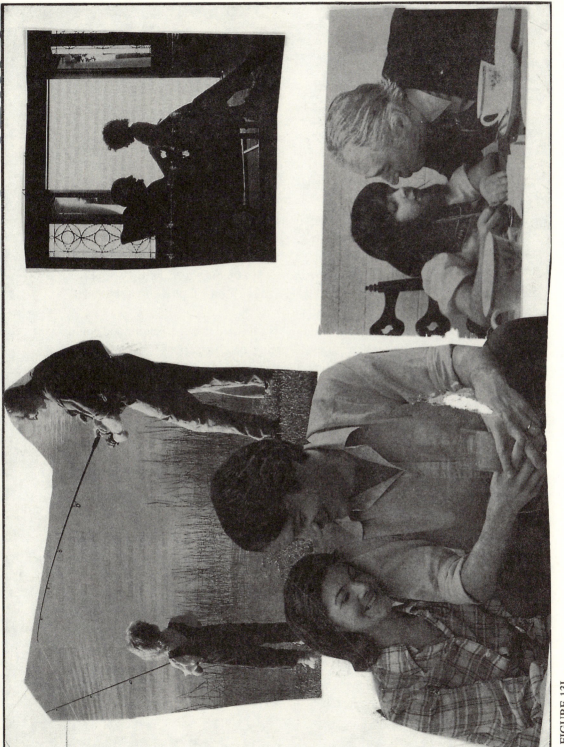

FIGURE 13I

Hispanic 11-Year-Old Male: Attention Deficit Disorder

Luis had been diagnosed with an Undifferentiated Attention Deficit Disorder. The school reported that he had a problem with concentration, spoke to his classmates when the teacher was giving instructions, had difficulty staying seated, was generally restless, and intruded upon other children's games. His reading and writing skills were far below average. Luis' test scores placed him in the low normal range of intelligence.

When he was interviewed, his conversation and projective drawings suggested more potential than was shown by his IQ tests. The MPC was used to evaluate the boy's abilities and to gain insight into his low self-esteem.

The procedure was presented in game-like fashion, with instructions to *pick out pictures that you like and paste them down on the paper.* Free associations were purposely omitted to avoid any perception of pressure for correct answers.

In contrast to his school behavior, Luis followed the instructions and could stay focused on the task without fidgeting or abstractions. The selection, placement, and pasting, were done adequately and within a reasonable length of time. When he hesitated, the boy referred to himself as a "dummy." He viewed the collage as harmless and unrelated to a mastery task.

The MPC (Figure 14A) included:

1. *A paper face.*
2. *A woman with the head of a cat.*
3. *Snapshot of a man that had been ripped into pieces then put back together.*
4. *A man and boy looking at a cockatoo.*

Comments. The photographs evoked some questions. What did the photograph of a torn snapshot that was put back together mean? What did the paper face of a person and the cat-faced human figure symbolize? It seemed the couple looking at the bird might stand for the boy and his father.

The MPC was puzzling and the hints that it encompassed were not clear.

In subsequent sessions, Luis created a number of similar collages where the people were never quite "real." These strange pictures led the therapist to wonder if the child had a thought disorder or if they were a metaphor for anger toward some significant person.

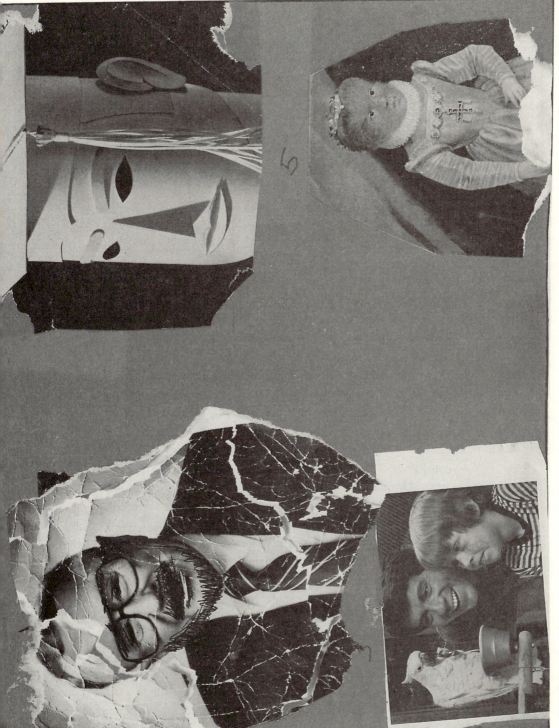

FIGURE 14A

It was not until the therapist had a conjoint session with Luis and his mother that the puzzle was answered. This parent lacked any affect. In a collage that the pair created together, the mother contributed only miscellaneous items that veered away from emotions. Her interactions with her son lacked warmth or caring.

In the next individual session, Luis's collage with the paper-face and cat woman was brought out. He was told, *look at these pictures and pretend how you would feel if you saw real people who looked like this.*

The MPC (Figure 14B) included:

1. *A ferocious wolf* meant, "It would make me mad because the lady with the cat face wouldn't be able to talk so I could understand. She would only talk like, meow, meow."
2. *A bear about to pounce* showed his response to the "paper-face." Luis related, "I'd be mad. I'd wanna tear up the paper face 'cause it's not right. A person should have real skin."
3. *A wild tiger* stood for reactions to the torn snapshot, "I'd be mad," he said, "cause it's not a real person, it's just a picture that someone tore up. I don't know why it got tore up."
4. *A wrestler* was another metaphor for his reaction to the cat-face woman: "When I'm mad I'd like to beat the weird person up."
5. *A wrestler (the same person as above) leaning against a wall, possibly praying,* represented, "If I hurt somebody, maybe I pray to God."

Comments. The collage gave Luis a safe place to ventilate and sublimate his anger toward his uninvolved mother. The *wolf* and *tiger* pictures expressed his frustration over his mother's lack of affect and her miscommunication. The *bear ready to pounce* is the enraged part of himself that reacts to the mask because it has no substance. The *two wrestlers* reveals both his rage and guilt toward his mother. The *man and boy* photograph was not responded to; a guess would be that his relationship with his father is positive. However, another guess about his father is related to the torn snapshot, which might represent Luis's anger that his father does not respond to his wife's inadequate mothering. However, without a family meeting, this speculation carries little weight.

In a large number of MPCs, Luis incorporated chaotic and destructive symbols. The photographs cited below were chosen in various sessions. They demonstrate the importance of pictorial thematic repetition that indicate concerns.

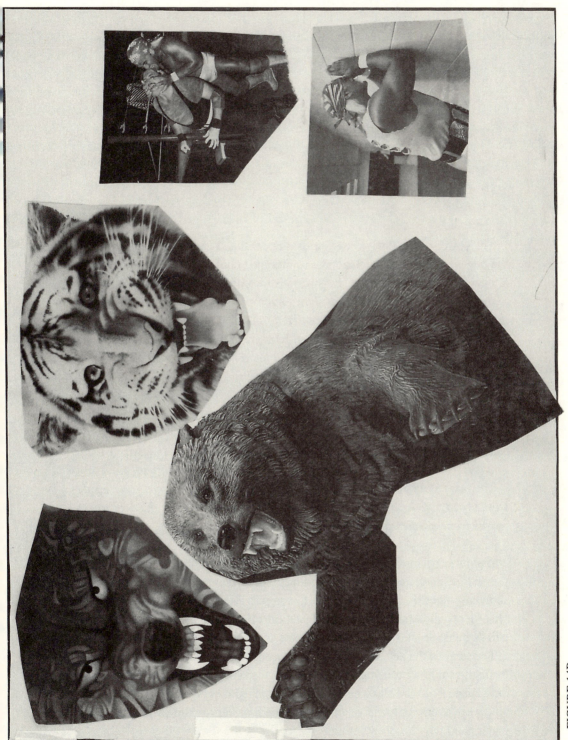

FIGURE 14B

1. *A wrecked home.*
2. *An accident.*
3. *A volcano.*
4. *A hand holding pills.*
5. *Broken glass.*
6. *Wild animals.*
7. *Soldiers shooting.*
8. *Police shooting.*
9. *A ship in a stormy sea.*
10. *Enraged people.*
11. *Knifes.*

The power of these nonverbal messages exhibited Luis's potent fury. Since the boy was not to be overloaded, the therapist chose only five collages containing the items listed above. Luis was instructed: *Look through these collages and cut out THREE pictures that show angry or scary things. Paste them onto the page and make up a story about each one.*

The boy responded with a quizzical look, yet set himself to the task. Luis chose the *volcano, a wrecked car, and a hand holding pills* (Figure 14C).

The first tale was: *A volcano that exploded because it had logs of lava inside. It was there for a very long time and it was time to blow because that's what volcanos are suppose to do.*

The second story related: *There was this man who was driving good and suddenly a car came out of a street and crashed into the man that was driving good. He didn't get bad hurt. He was lucky but he was very mad.*

The third story was: *There is this lady person who didn't feel good inside so she went into the medicine chest and took some pills. I think she has cancer because she smokes a lot.*

Comments. The first story of the VOLCANO was equivalent to Luis's repressed feelings. Perhaps, he wished that like a volcano he could explode and show his anger that he kept inside. It was possible that the Attention Deficit Disorder symptoms were a manifestation of his concealed emotions. The child's behavior in therapy was opposite to that exhibited in school.

The story of the accident with the "innocent victim" seemed related to Luis. He had trouble with being identified being in "special education" and as the only Hispanic in the classroom. Luis complained that he was unlike his peers who were overly aggressive and oppositional or very withdrawn. He did not understand why he was there.

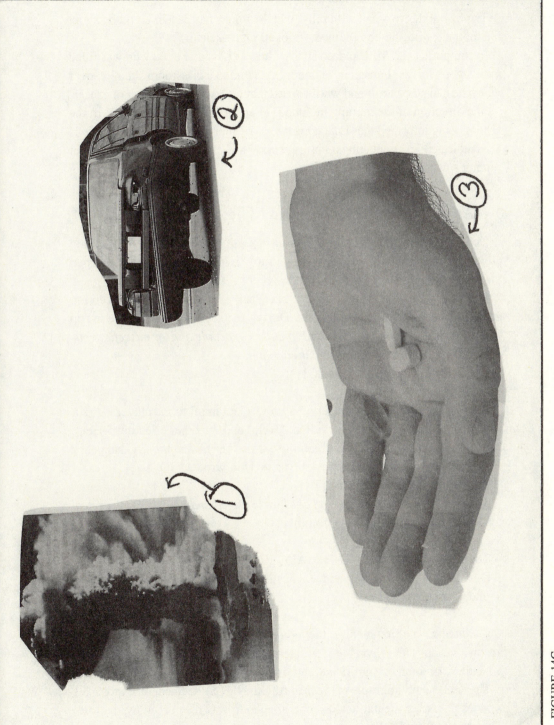

FIGURE 14C

The tale of the "woman with pills" who he thinks has cancer could be about his mother, who, he complained, smoked a great deal.

In composite, the MPC placed strong clues to Luis as a child who was filled with rage; who saw himself as an innocent victim in a classroom situation over which he had no control; and who worried that his mother was dying of cancer.

The direction of the therapy included: a) an increase in self-esteem; b) the school being informed that Luis appeared to be more intelligent than previous tests indicated; c) conducting a family session and clarifying Luis's fears about mother's cancer.

Asian-American 15-Year-Old Male: Fear of Psychosis

Don was adopted at birth. He was attractive, bright, and an outstanding athlete. His parents requested group therapy in hopes that it would sharpen his socialization skills.

Don was placed in a time-limited, six-week assessment and intervention group for adolescent boys and girls. During the second meeting, the group was told: *Pick out and paste THREE pictures of people and/or miscellaneous items. Then, state something about each person.*

Don's MPC (Figure 15A) included:

1. *A football game* with a *referee* saying, "Cool man" to the players. Also, *two football players.* One yelled, "Help" and the other cried out, "Help, I need somebody." By mistake, the words *"Verified capability"* happened to be left on the photograph. Over it, Don wrote, "BO" [*sic*].
2. *Brains* was captioned "NUT."
3. A *newborn baby whose navel cord was severed and held up with surgical scissors* was left without comments.

The MPC was entitled, THE MAD PICTURE.

Don used a felt marker and encapsulated each image with a scribbly boundary line.

Comments. The first picture, the *football player* crying for help, alluded to his own needs. The *referee's* encouragement might be symbolic of his coach, his father, or another significant authority figure.

The second photograph of *brains* (titled NUTS) seemed to expose his worries about his mental health. This innuendo was reinforced by the title, THE MAD PICTURE.

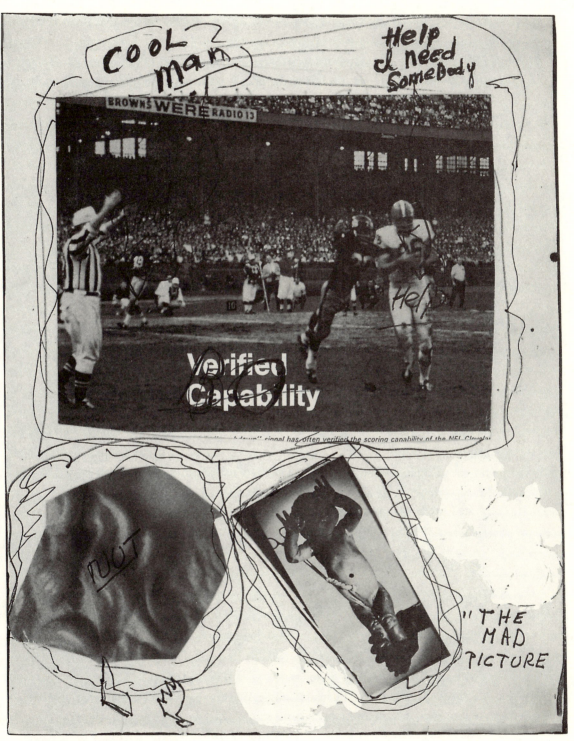

FIGURE 15A

The third image, of the *newborn baby,* might be related to the question of his biological mother.

The MPC's poignant statement was taken seriously. Disturbing free associations and the need to encapsulate each photo were strong clues that pointed to serious psychopathology. The collage shows Don's pervasive worry of being psychotic.

The support that he received from the other adolescents in the group was a comfort to him. He was surprised that he could admit his fears in a group setup and still be accepted.

In addition to group therapy, individual treatment was recommended.

Black 17-Year-Old Male: Gender Identity Confusion

Jim was the youngest of four children in an intact family. His parents reported him as oppositional; he stayed out late at night and refused to tell his parents where he had been. He was known to participate in street gang fights. Jim was caught stealing cans of spray paint. When questioned by the police, he proudly admitted to being a graffiti artist whose work was displayed on buildings and under freeways. A sheriff's diversion program placed him on probation with the provision that he receive therapy.

First Session

Jim was belligerent and made "whitey," remarks to the therapist. He was irate that his therapist was a middle-class Caucasian woman who he believed could not understand him or his problems.

He was antagonistic toward the clinician and to therapy. Since he was interested in visual imagery, a decision was made to include the MPC.

During the initial session, Jim was instructed: *Pick out pictures that interest you and paste them down. Then, write something about each picture.*

The MPC (Figure 16A) included:

1. *George Washington.* With felt markers, the *hair* was darkened and *a beard, mustache, and eyeglasses* were added, plus the features were outlined.
2. *A hand holding up lipstick* was positioned near Washington's lips, along with the words, "great flavor."
3. *A large eye* was pasted beneath George Washington. When asked what the collage meant, Jim laughed and said, "The Washington idea was a lie. George Washington was probably a liar. Besides guys like that will probably get AIDS."

FIGURE 16A

Comments. Although Jim's MPC was intended as a "shock tactic," he unknowingly divulged a good deal of himself. It was plausible that the collage alluded to his sexual identity confusion. He may also be threatened by homosexuality and the possibility of contracting AIDS.

Third Session

Two weeks later, Jim was given another *free choice* collage option. The MPC (Figure 16B) included:

1. *A large screw.*
2. *A bottle of liquor.*
3. *A Black man holding out his forefinger.* Jim situated the *man* as if he were emerging out of the picture of the liquor bottle. Jim drew a line that connected *the man's finger* to the *screw.* He titled the MPC, THE TAMING OF THE SCREW.

Comments. As Jim created the collage, he grinned and glanced at the therapist to check out her reactions. He wanted to see if she would be stunned at, or could understand, or could tolerate the theme of his collage. It was through humor that his fears and conflicts were hinted at.

Another clue might be in the *liquor bottle.* Perhaps alcohol abuse was being intimated.

Jim was astonished and relieved when the therapist addressed the issues of homosexuality and masturbation. He felt understood in spite of the cultural differences that existed between them.

Caucasian 21-Year-Old Male: Drug Abuse

Rick was placed on probation by the court, due to his drug dealing.

During the first six weeks of treatment, Rick's MPCs were not unusual. He was deliberately cautious in his vocal and visual statements. He claimed that he was reformed and had nothing to do with drugs anymore.

During the seventh week in therapy, Rick produced two significant collages. The MPCs included:

1. *A Caucasian male portrait of a forehead, eyes, and nose* (the rest was cut off) (Figure 17A). With a felt marker he added *a head of hair, a lipsticked mouth, and red eyes. Facial lines* were augmented, as well as

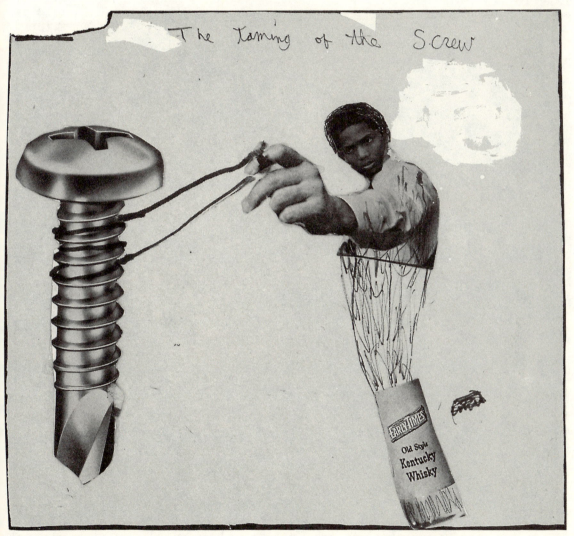

FIGURE 16B

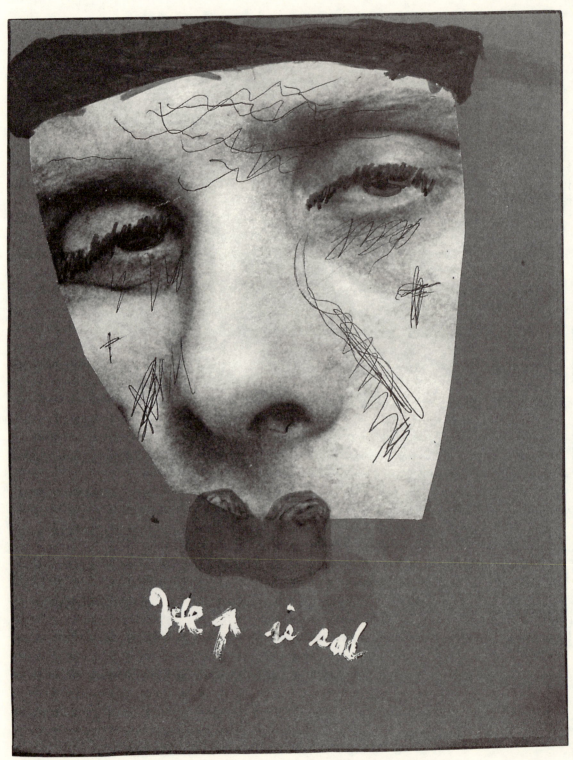

FIGURE 17A

a *cross on each cheek.* Below it he wrote, "He is sad."

2. *A man's portrait* (Figure 17B). With a red marker Rick colored in the *pupils* and added *a head of hair, a mustache, and a beard.* He had the man saying, "LSD? WHATS LSD?"

3. Upon *a Caucasian man* he drew *glasses, a hat, red nostrils, and uplifted eyebrows.* The man was saying, "COKE? STUIPID [*sic*] PUNKS."

Comments. These MPCs had a recognizably bizarre quality, one that is frequently presented by schizophrenics and/or persons in the midst of a drug-induced psychosis.

Rick, stripped of his defenses, unconsciously spilled out his distorted perceptions and revealed the effect drugs had on him. Without the protection of his defense mechanism, he went so far as to name the two drugs that he had taken. An immediate confrontation was pursued. In subsequent sessions, the MPCs were used to understand his nonverbalized mental states.

Caucasian, Jewish, 28-Year-Old Female: Individuation

Sara was the only child of a Holocaust survivor's family. Both her parents and remaining grandparents had been interned in German concentration camps. Recently, she was offered a position with a prestigious law firm. If she accepted it, a move to a distant state was required.

Sara described her relationships with her parents as "very loving and very close." Because of her ambivalence about accepting the job, she sought brief therapy. If the position were accepted, she would leave in six weeks. It was agreed that the brief intervention would be focused on her difficulty in making a critical career decision.

First Session

To begin the brief service intervention, the therapist instructed Sara: *Pick out pictures that catch your attention and paste them down. Then free associate to the images.*

The MPC (Figure 18A) contained:

1. A *pleased little Caucasian girl on a jungle gym* was associated with, "If this girl is not careful, she might get hurt badly."

2. The *car-testing dummy* elicited the comment, "A seat belt is an important safety factor."

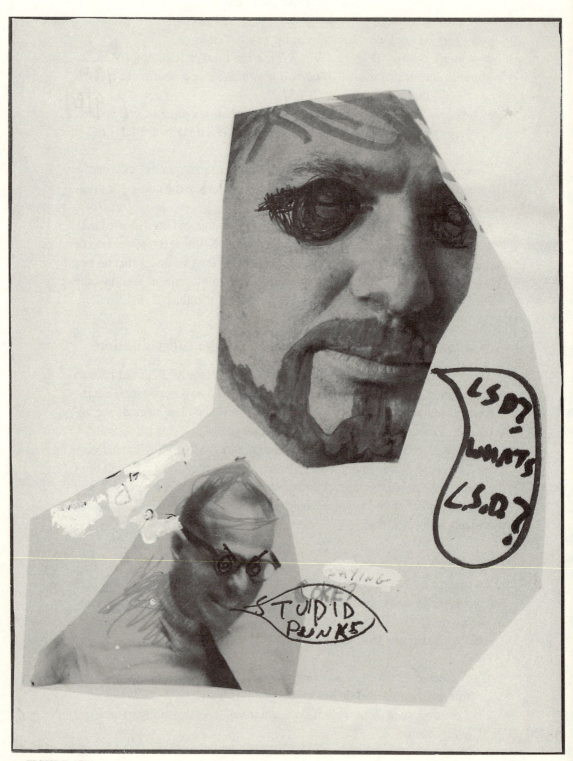

FIGURE 17B

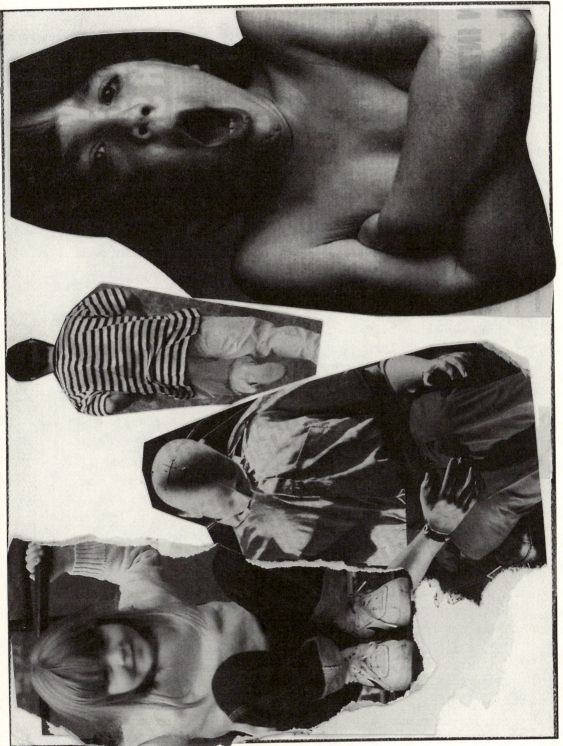

FIGURE 18A

3. *A Caucasian person running* brought about, "Running fast is hard on the back and knees because of the hard impact on the body. Swimming is better exercise."

4. *A nude Caucasian child hugging his body and yawning* was accompanied with, "If he doesn't put his clothes on right away, he could catch pneumonia."

Sophisticated Sara laughed when she saw the consistent message about "THE WORLD OF DANGERS," as she so aptly titled it. The rest of the session was taken up with the way the women in her family were so protective of her. They were fearful of a catastrophic happening. Although the hidden meanings were subtly related, they were often repeated. Sara recalled incidents of her mother's warnings, "Be careful darling, watch out for yourself." These messages were given not only in the past, but also in the present.

Second Session

Sara was instructed: *Select pictures of people who represent members of your family. Then, tell what they often say to you.*

The MPC (Figure 18B) included:

1. *A Caucasian man and child watching fish in a tank* represented her father who often said, "Let's do a good job with cleaning out the fish tank. Then we can go and buy ice cream, dearie."

2. *An old Caucasian man* was a metaphor for her grandfather who frequently told her, "Come here my sweet one, so I can give you a big hug and a kiss. Here's some money so you can buy yourself something you like."

3. *An old Caucasian woman, walking while she is in pain,* stood for her grandmother who often warned her: "Be careful!" "Watch yourself." "Don't get hit by a car when you are crossing the street." "Don't eat too fast or you might choke." "Don't talk to strangers, they could kidnap you."

4. The *smiling Caucasian woman setting forth some fancy jello* symbolized her mother, who called out to her, "Come eat this nice food that I made just for you, because I love you so much. Then you can go out and play. But remember darling, be careful of the dog next door."

Once again Sara saw the stark evidence of the communications she received from her mother and grandmother. She had been aware of this phenomenon

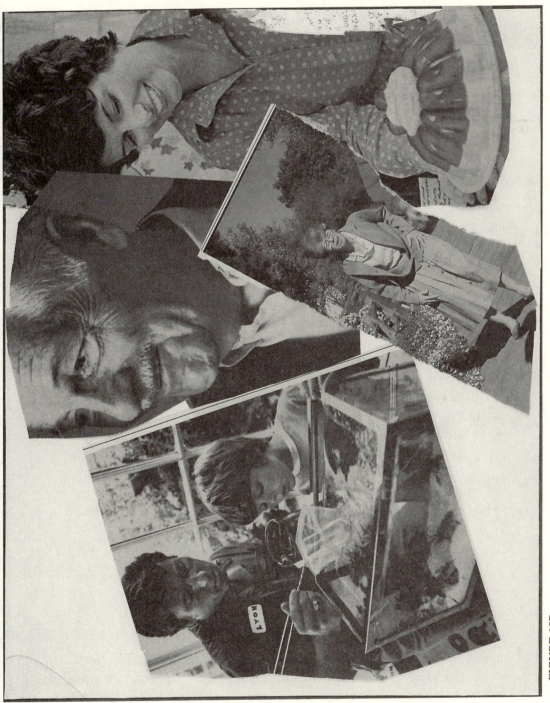

FIGURE 18B

before, but by seeing it in aggregate, she gained greater clarity and insight. It was plain to see that despite the women's loving messages, seeds of fear were planted.

Sara acknowledged that her ambivalence about her job change was connected not only to her apprehension of a new environment, but also to a concern about being separated from her family.

Third Session

It was apparent that some of Sara's indecision was due to the guilt of leaving her parents. This is a common experience for children of Holocaust survivors, especially when they are an only child. They tend to feel guilty because of their belief that they were destined to compensate for the horrendous family losses.

To deal with this issue, the directive was: *pick out any type of pictures that portray what makes you feel guilty.* Sara immediately requested a large sheet of paper, knowing that, "I'll be picking out a lot of pictures." She looked for symbols that would describe the guilt-provoking subjects.

The MPC (Figure 18C) included:

1. *An airplane* that meant, "flying away from the family."
2. *A dirty old shoe* represented, "the homeless people."
3. *The fetus,* the metaphor, "the fact that I am childless."
4. *A hand setting in a part of a puzzle* stood for, "I don't have all of the parts of my life together. I'm not married and the man I love wouldn't be approved of by my family. My parents don't even know about him."
5. *The plaster cast of a brain* exemplified, "when I lose a court case, I beat myself up and wonder if I had left anything undone."
6. *Salad* denoted, "If I don't eat all of the wonderful food that my mother and grandmother go through a lot of work to make, I feel terrible."
7. *A tool smoothing out cement* signified that, "I act as the cement that keeps it all together for my family. If I'm not there for them, I'm not certain what will happen."
8. *A crumbled note with the words "To Do"* on it indicated, "the necessity to keep up with my workload."
9. The *heart* embodied, "my father's heart disease."
10. *A smiling girl's face* characterized, "I feel guilty if I don't act all smiley and happy when I'm with my family." This final picture was unconsciously placed on top of a heart.

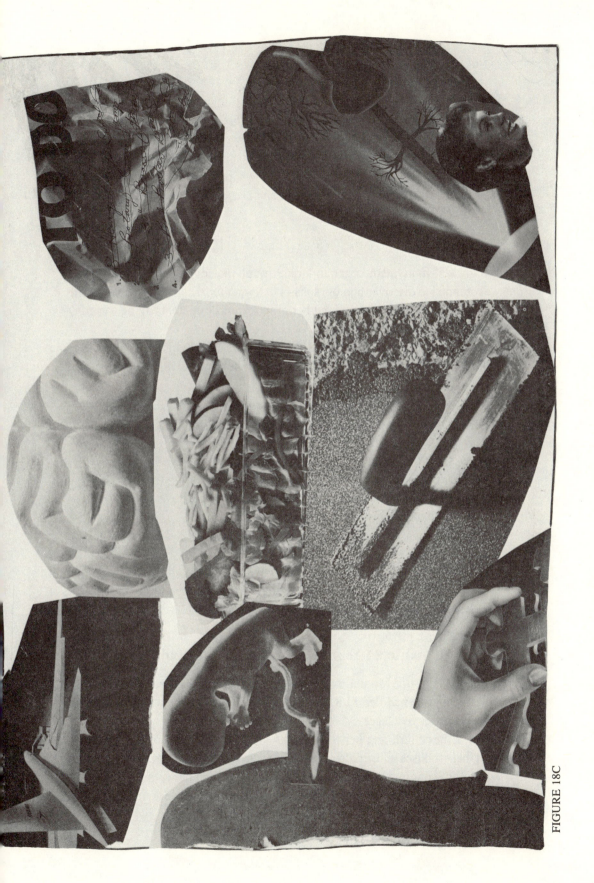

FIGURE 18C

Although Sara previously knew all the things that made her feel guilty, it was painful to see them so plainly through the MPCs. Fully aware of the collages' meaning, she explained that she usually compartmentalized each issue and had never before experienced them as such a "tight cluster."

Sara pointed out her *pictorial slip* about the happy face that was placed upon the heart. She confessed her fear that if she caused her father stress he might have a heart attack.

Fourth Session

Sara, self-motivated, began to look through the collage box of people and was stunned to discover photographs of *a Jewish funeral* and *a cemetery*. She confessed that any thoughts about her grandparents or parents dying someday were always pushed away.

Sara gathered courage and used the two pictures to help her face and deal with the issue of death of the older generations (Figure 18D).

Fifth Session

On her own, Sara decided to construct a DECISION collage.
The MPC (Figure 18E) included:

1. *A set of suitcases* represented an obvious declaration to leave.
2. *A signpost with arrows going in all directions with the words RISK on all of them* designated her current situation.
3. *A bridge* was a positive symbol for "bridging myself to a new and exciting job and life."

Comments. The last MPC demonstrated Sara's decision to go ahead with the change and to bring closure to the brief service intervention.

Hispanic 34-Year-Old Woman: Guilt Expiation

Maya had a son, Miguel, who was 14 years of age and had been born out of wedlock. She had fled El Salvador with her boy when he was five and was married just a year ago.

Maya, her child, and her husband lived with her family of origin, along with their spouses and children. This integrated living arrangement was preferred for economic and emotional reasons. Maya and her spouse, as well as other family members, were ambitious and hoped to remove themselves from menial jobs.

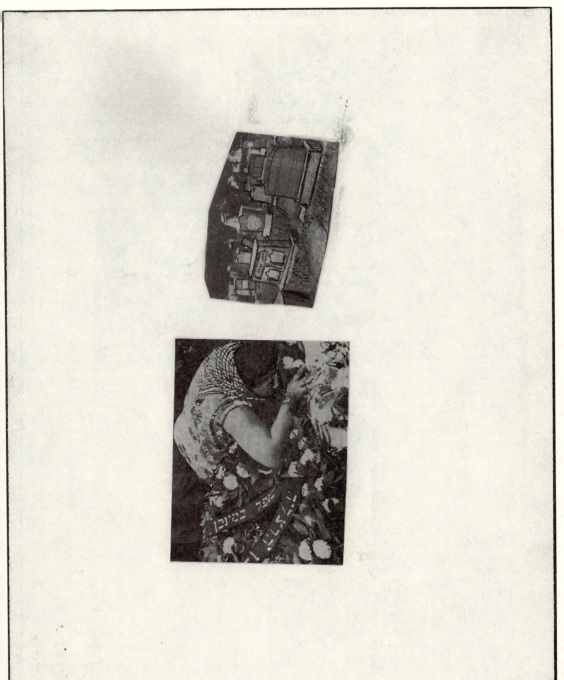

FIGURE 18D

FIGURE 18E

The client worked as a full-time housekeeper. Her employer noticed Maya's recent depleted energy and asked her if she was pregnant. Although a "No" response brought on tears, Maya refused to discuss the matter.

In the weeks that followed, the employer became increasingly concerned about Maya. She was sad most of the time, had lost her motivation, and was arriving late to work. Hence, an ultimatum was given to either to seek therapy at a clinic or find another job.

Maya began treatment reluctantly because of her poor English and unfamiliarity with therapy. She also believed that the American-born Caucasian therapist would not understand her because of language and cultural barriers.

When the MPC technique was presented, Maya grasped that she might express herself through pictures even where language could fail her. Initially, the collages were directed to her own household. They displayed her happiness within the family setting. She portrayed contentment in having many members at hand to help with the child care. Numerous collages were filled with photographs of *food*. These demonstrated that with so many people working, there was always an abundance of nourishment. Other illustrations indicated the significance of having caring people close by, with whom she could share her problems.

By the time Maya had expressed all of the above, her qualms about the culturally different therapist had disappeared. Thereafter, the directives became explicit and required more intimate information. They encompassed her attitudes about specific family members; the problems with her living conditions; difficulties inherent in cultural change; and feelings that revolved around her job and employers.

As the therapeutic alliance was strengthened, Maya was instructed: *Pick out pictures of things that worry* (molestar) *you.*

The MPC (Figure 19A) contained:

1. *The design of a face and a hand holding up a test tube.*
2. *A surgeon.*
3. *A surgeon performing an operation on a young girl.*
4–5. *Two young children in diapers.*

When the collage was finished, Maya began to cry. Torn up emotionally, she was unable to talk about the MPC, yet continued to create another collage.

This MPC (Figure 19B) included:

1. *Pretzels in a dish.*

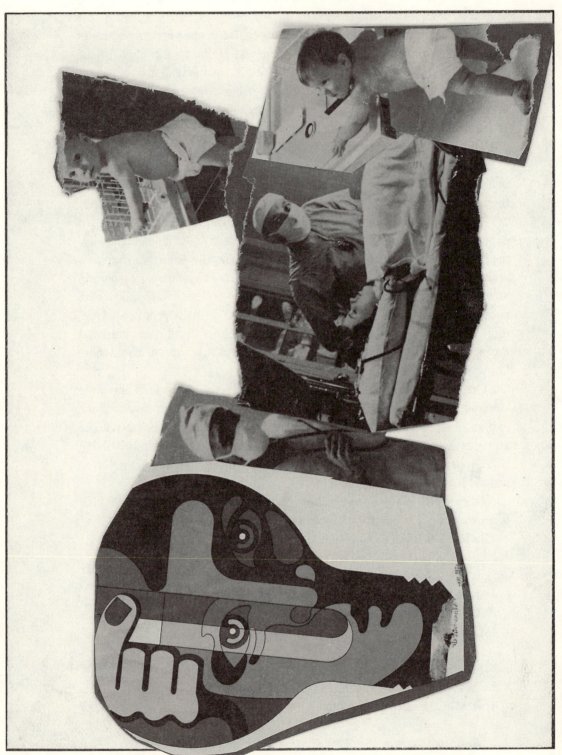

FIGURE 19A

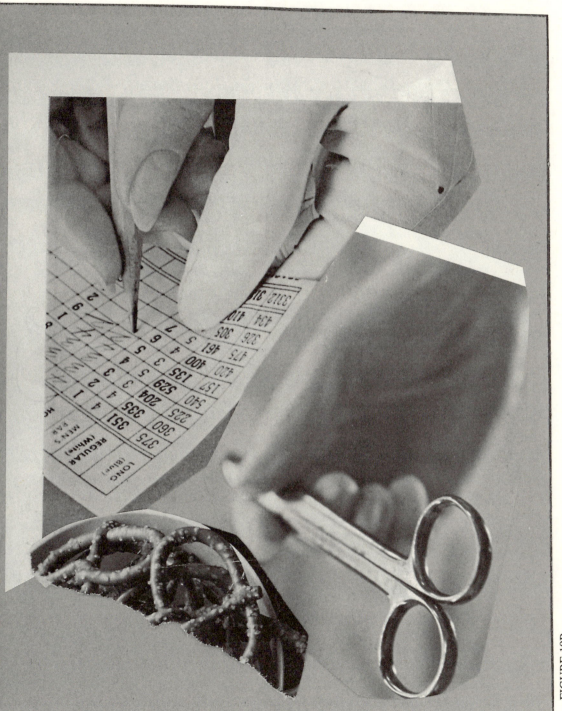

FIGURE 19B

2. *A rubber-gloved hand handing over a surgical scissors.*
3. *The two hands of a medical person. One is gloved while the other is charting.*

Sadly, Maya looked up to see if the therapist understood her message. It was answered with the speculation that maybe *she* had undergone surgery. Maya nodded in agreement and was quick to make another collage. This time a poignant story was related through the photographs.

The MPC (Figure 19C) contained:

1. *A pregnant woman with a set of eyes superimposed upon the belly.*
2. *A large eye behind reading glasses.*
3. *A Hispanic man.*

Maya was still teary eyed and embarrassed when she began to share her *secreto.* She revealed that 10 months after her first son was born, while she was still unwed, she was made pregnant again by the same man. He was married and furious with her request for "child support." When he began to curse and scream profanities at her, Maya became enraged and in her attempt to throw an object at him, lost her balance and fell over. She bled profusely and was rushed to a hospital where the baby was spontaneously aborted. Her guilt over this event was still with her.

Maya explained that her husband now wanted a child. Although they had sex frequently, she had not gotten pregnant. She was convinced that she was being punished by God because of her past.

After this confession, Maya began to feel more relaxed, but she was unaware of the reason. In the following weeks, she reported that intercourse had somehow become more satisfying.

After a few months, Maya ecstatically announced that she was going to have a baby. Even as therapy came to an end, she never made the connection between her confession, the expiation of guilt, and her ability to get pregnant.

Asian 40-Year-Old Female: Schizophrenic

Misu, a second-generation Japanese-American woman, was hospitalized and diagnosed as schizophrenic. The MPC was used as a tool for revealing her unconscious. Primitive aspects of schizophrenics usually spill out through their metaphoric images, which yield the patient's illusional or delusional systems.

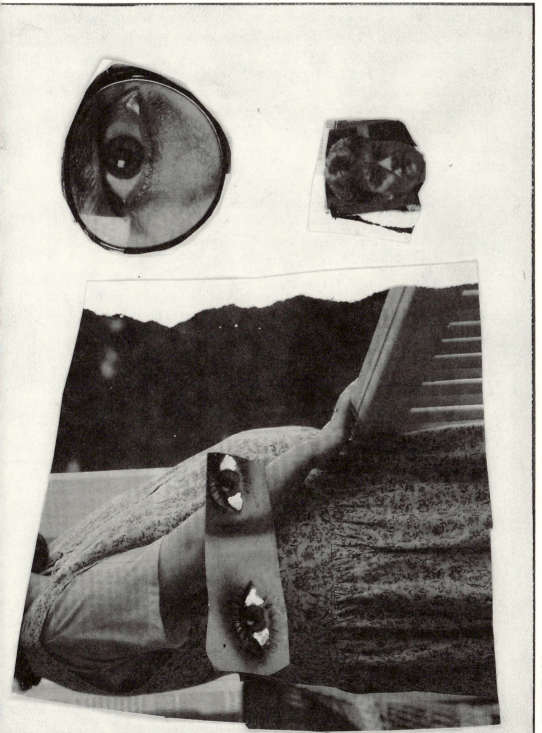

FIGURE 19C

The MPC was used along with Misu's multiple therapies. During the first session she was told: *Pick out pictures and paste them onto the paper. Then write or talk about the meanings.*

Misu's process was loose and unstructured. She was unable to stop herself from picking out an excessive amount of photographs. Parts of bodies were cut away and eyes were cut or torn out and glued randomly across the entire page. Great quantities of glue were slopped onto the MPC, the table, and herself as well.

The MPC (Figure 20A) included:

1-11. *Men and women from various cultures plus body parts.*
   12. *A dead tree.*
   13. *A Caucasian telephone man climbing up a post.*
   14. *A multiplicity of faces, eyes, superimposed on various places.*

With a felt marker, Misu encapsulated many of the images and scribbled over others. Her free associations poured out, and were at times incoherent.

It was obvious that the client required containment. In the next session, a metaphoric "holding environment" was provided through media restrictions. Paper size was reduced, photograph selection diminished to 10 pictures, and a gluestick substituted for liquid glue.

The instructions for the second MPC were: *Make a collage out of only TWO pictures. Then, write or talk about what they mean.*

Misu still had trouble with limiting herself and picked out five images. To help her stay within the set boundaries, the therapist removed the other five photos.

She was then instructed: *Pick out TWO pictures that you like and paste them down. Then, write or talk about their meaning.* As soon as two photographs were chosen, the rest were set aside by the therapist.

The MPC (Figure 20B) included:

1. *A bottle of Listerine mouthwash* with the words underneath, "She needs." Next to it, she printed, "MY MOUTHER" [*sic*].
2. *A person in an old English costume* with a *large eye* that replaced the *head.* The statement, "She (Mother) looks like this," was placed near it.

Once again Misu encapsulated the pictures. Before the collage was completed, she lost control and randomly cut out pieces from the entire page. The client believed that this action enhanced the collage.

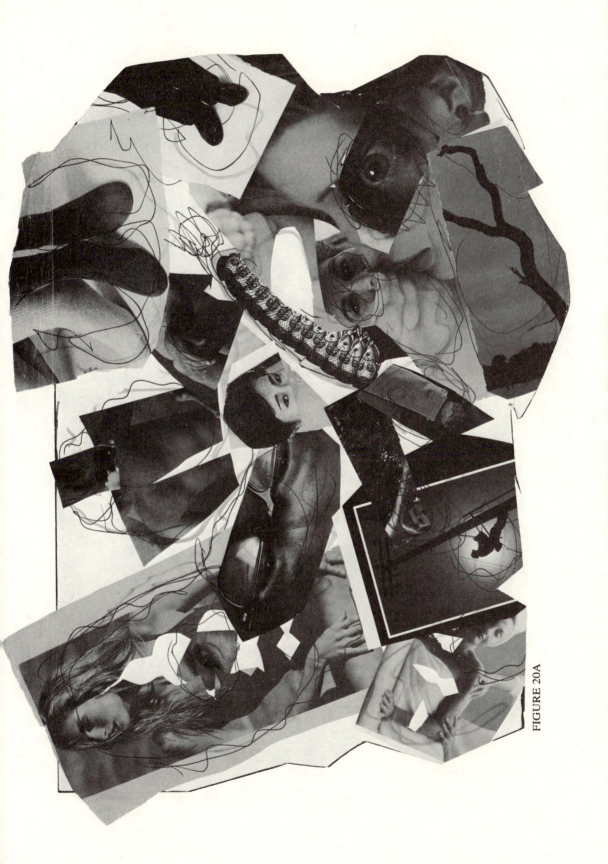

FIGURE 20A

FIGURE 20B

The next task was, again: *Choose only TWO pictures.* This time the image selection was reduced to five, and again the client needed help to constrain herself.

The MPC (Figure 20C) contained:

1. *A Caucasian woman. Arrows* were drawn into the picture and labeled MY MOUTHER [*sic*].
2. *A Caucasian man's back with nails all over the lower part of his body,* upon which she superimposed an *eye* (this illustration hung halfway off the page).

As a finishing touch, Misu included an "impingement feature" when she drew *arrows into the sides of the body.* She ended by making scissor cuts on the page at large.

Comments. The bizarre quality of the MPCs verified Misu's nonfunctional state. A consultation with a psychiatrist led to an adjustment of her medication.

With a correction in medication, Misu was better able to perform on a higher cognitive level. An example of the change is shown when the first task was repeated. The same instructions were given: *Pick out pictures and paste them onto the paper. Then, write or talk about what they mean.* The only difference in the materials was that she was given a gluestick instead of liquid glue.

The MPC (Figure 20D) included:

1–6. *Asian people with a variety of expression on their faces.*
7–8. *The eyes and ears of an Asian woman.*
   9. *A Black man* brought the remarks, "He looks very sexy and strong. I could go for a man like that."

Comments. These collages were more organized and the content coherent. Only the picture of the eyes and ears might hint at sensory hallucinations or perhaps some paranoia.

It was only when Misu was more reality-oriented that she used mostly Asian images with which she could identify.

The MPCs served to reveal Misu's illusions and at times forewarned her regression.

Asian 44-Year-Old Male: Psychosomatic Symptoms

Yens had been sent by his Japanese, Osaka-based company to work in the United States. Previously, he had spent a few years in California while attending graduate school.

MY MOUTHER

FIGURE 20C

FIGURE 20D

The client had complained of trouble with his eyes and frequent headaches. Medical examinations indicated a caffeine addiction. Although Yens managed to withdraw from coffee, he still suffered from the same psychosomatic symptoms. For this reason, and due to his tremendous work pressures, he requested "stress reduction therapy." The client was referred for biofeedback and group therapy.

The group was dynamically oriented and usually began with a MPC as a warmup technique. It gave the members a catalyst for their self exploration. Each week the sessions began with the same instructions: *Select one or two pictures of people or miscellaneous items and paste them down. Then write anything that comes to mind about the picture.*

The collages that Yens produced in group therapy during the first seven weeks of therapy are reported below.

First Session

In the first group session, Yens looked uncomfortable when he saw he was the only Asian present. Fearful about therapy, he knew he would be expected to express himself openly.

Yens was puzzled when magazine photographs were put out. A participant explained the MPC procedure. When everyone began to look over the pictures, he reluctantly joined them.

Yens' MPC (Figure 21A) included:

1. *A woman.*
2. *A dog.*
3. The *dog's face and one leg* were cut out and replaced with those same parts of the *woman.* It was captioned, THINKING OF DOGMA.

The participants got a good laugh out of the collage and it brought positive attention to Yens.

Second Session

As Yens was the first person to enter the room, he looked uncertain about remaining. However, as the other members soon followed, he took a seat. When everyone began their collages, he, too, became involved.

Yens' MPC (Figure 21B) included:

1. *An Asian man.*
2. A second *Asian man,* who says, SCIENTICICLY [*sic*] SPEAKING.

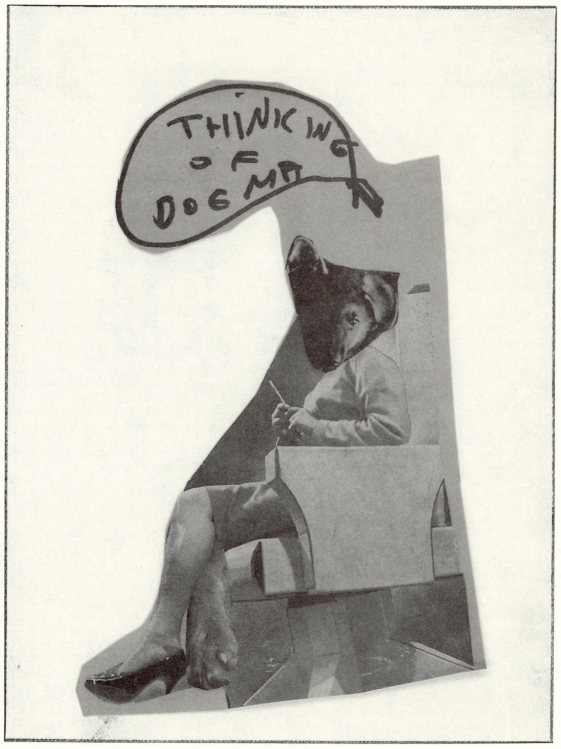

FIGURE 21A

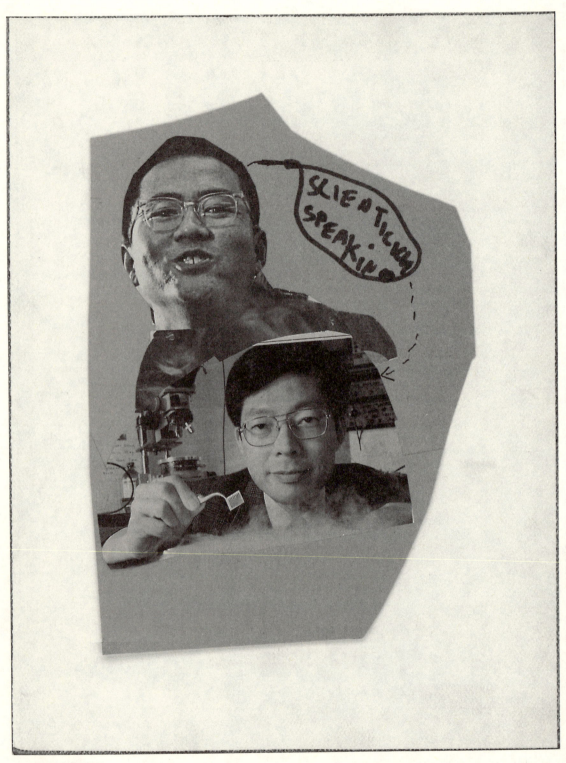

FIGURE 21B

The group enjoyed having Yens as a member because of his knack for lightening up their spirits. However, the therapist recognized his resistance to exposing himself. It may have been exacerbated by the group of Caucasian strangers. Yens cleverly used humor as a defense by camouflaging his problems through visual jokes.

Third Session

The group was jovial as they greeted Yens. Several people complimented him on his past collages. It encouraged him to create the next one.
Yens' MPC (Figure 21C) contained:

1. *Three penguins.*
2. *Three portraits of Asian persons were superimposed upon penguins' faces.* It was captioned, ALL DRESSED UP AND GOING NOWHERE.

The attention that Yens received made him a "star."

Fourth Session

Yens was in a good mood. He was confident about his comic role in group.
Yens' MPC (Figure 21D) included:

1. *Four birds in a nest.*
2. *Four faces of Asian children* were superimposed upon the *bird's faces.* The photograph showed three of the birds huddled together. This grouping was labeled, BIRDS OF A FEATHER. The fourth bird was titled, HE WILL HAVE FLU [*sic*] THE COUP [*sic*].

As usual, the collage delighted the group. Yens received positive reinforcement for getting the members to laugh. Nevertheless, one woman wondered aloud, "Who really flew the coop?" But the remark was ignored.

Fifth Session

As the meeting began, several people mentioned that they looked forward to seeing Yen's collage.
Yens' MPC (Figure 21E) included:

1. *Two seals leaning against each other.*
2. *Portraits of a Japanese man and a blonde Caucasian woman* were

FIGURE 21C

FIGURE 21D

FIGURE 21E

superimposed upon the faces of the seals. It was labeled, HE FLIPPED
OVER HER.

The group appreciated the MPC. One member said Yens could always be
counted on to bring a light touch into their heavy sessions. However, one
woman said, "I wonder about the real people behind the human-headed seals."
When an answer was not forthcoming, she noted his pattern not to reveal
himself. She added that even though Yens was "fun," his avoidance of personal
statements was resented.

In agreement, another person supported these comments. He referred to
Yens as an "observer and humorist," rather then "a working member of the
group."

Yens, taken by surprise, was shaken by the encounter. He remained silent
for the rest of the session.

Sixth Session

Yens phoned in to say he was unable to attend the group because he had "the
flu." Although the members were regretful, someone joked that Yens, like his
collage, "flew the coop."

Seventh Session

When Yens returned, he confessed that the confrontation had upset him.
Admitting that it was hard for him to come back to group, he said he felt
embarrassed and exposed. Yet, he bravely decided to explain the significance
behind his joking collages.

He referred back to his first MPC, of the "woman with the head of a bear."
The group was reminded that it was titled DOGMA. He said the hidden
meaning referred to his father's "dogmatic attitude toward my mother and us
children."

Although Yens stated it was culturally based, he found it troublesome since
he had adopted American ideas and standards. He disclosed that it pained him
to see how his mother catered to his father in an old-fashioned humble way.

With the group's empathic response, Yens went on to unmask the BIRDS
OF A FEATHER collage. He disclosed that three of the human-faced birds
huddled together represented his siblings, while the fourth bird symbolized
himself, who was "trying to fly the coop."

Yens confessed that the collage of the seals with Japanese and Caucasian
faces represented his girlfriend and himself. After these disclosures, the group
created their weekly collages.

Yens' MPC (Figure 21F) included:

1. *An Asian man plus a Caucasian woman dressed in white.* He announced it stood for his wish to break away from family tradition and to get brave enough to marry his Caucasian girlfriend.

The group was appreciative of Yens' explanations. It opened up a discussion about their own problems with interracial and interethnic relationships. Individuals also addressed their struggles with pleasing or rebelling against their parents' value system.

Comments. Yens found the group's empathy and support to be an entirely new experience for him. Never before had he expressed himself so openly. This unique and culturally different episode helped him to trust the members of the group.

In the following meetings, Yens was able to explore many issues and emotions that had formerly been covered up. As he began to feel better physically, he understood the connection between his state of mind and the effects it had upon his body.

Mixed-Cultures Women's Group Ages 32–54: Sexual Issues

A women's group was composed of individuals from various cultures. Their ages ranged from 32 through 54. The members sought therapy for a variety of reasons. Meetings were conducted in a classical verbal psychotherapy approach. Because the group had reached a plateau, the MPC was implemented as a catalyst.

The first task required the participants to portray *Where I Came From.* Some of the MPC responses were:

1. *A shopping spree* that Rene, a Caucasian woman, had taken on the way to the session (Figure 22A).
2. *A trash can* was chosen by Rethia, a Black woman, to represent the "rotten garbage neighborhood" that she was raised in (Figure 22B).
3. *A large Hispanic family* showed Celina's background (Figure 22C).

The most poignant collage, one that moved the members to tears and helped them deal with their own issues, belonged to Susan, Caucasian and 43 years of age.

FIGURE 21F

FIGURE 22A

FIGURE 22B

FIGURE 22C

Susan's MPC (Figure 22D) included:

1. *A Caucasian man with a hostile grimace holding up his fist* was accompanied by the words, "Anger at this."
2. *Fish in a tank* symbolized, "Fishbowl, crowded, poor, coldness of my childhood."
3. *A snake* represented having been, "Unloved, left, and struck at."
4. *Soldiers resting* stood for, "War and Confusion, poorly adjusted people that existed in my family."

Susan had always been an extremely verbal person in group. Her meaningless detailed reports layered over any personal issues. Although members were supportive of each other, they found that Susan irritated them. They changed their opinion when she shared the collage and gave her their empathy for the first time.

Since Susan was touched by the group's response, in the next meeting she dared to look deeper into herself through a *free choice* MPC. The collage that was titled SEX AND INHIBITIONS embodied the following (Figure 22E):

1. *A Caucasian man's torso with clenched fists and a large eye that replaced his head.* "Don't like," was written nearby, and "They watch," by the eye.
2. The *beautiful blond woman lying on her side* was accompanied by the word, "seductive."
3. The *faces of various people with all sorts of expressions* represented, "Do's and don'ts."
4. The *telephone poles and wires,* with its inference to sex, symbolized, "Tangled ideas!"

This MPC astonished the participants. They were sympathetic and since many of them could relate to this issue, it caused the group to look into themselves.

Comments. Susan's MPC about sex gave her a vehicle to explore her childhood and her marital life. Looking at the role she played with her husband was a pivotal part of her therapy.

The topic of sexual aspects of relationships opened up the entire group to examine this vital issue, which had previously been avoided.

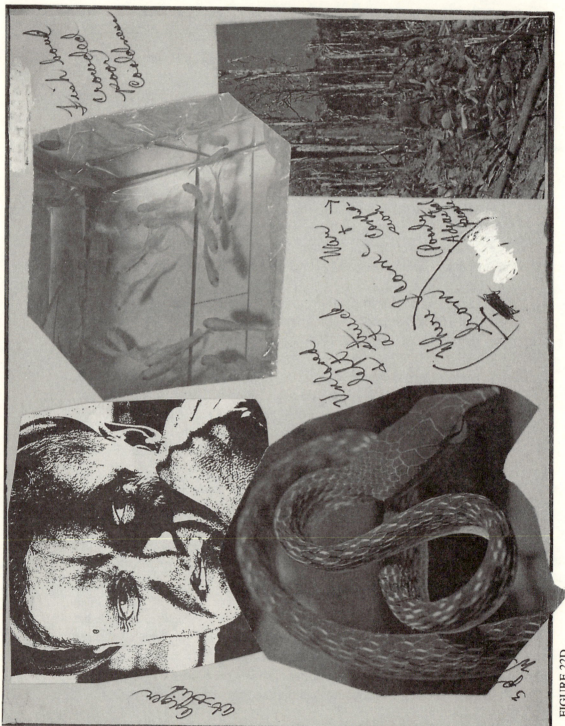

FIGURE 22D

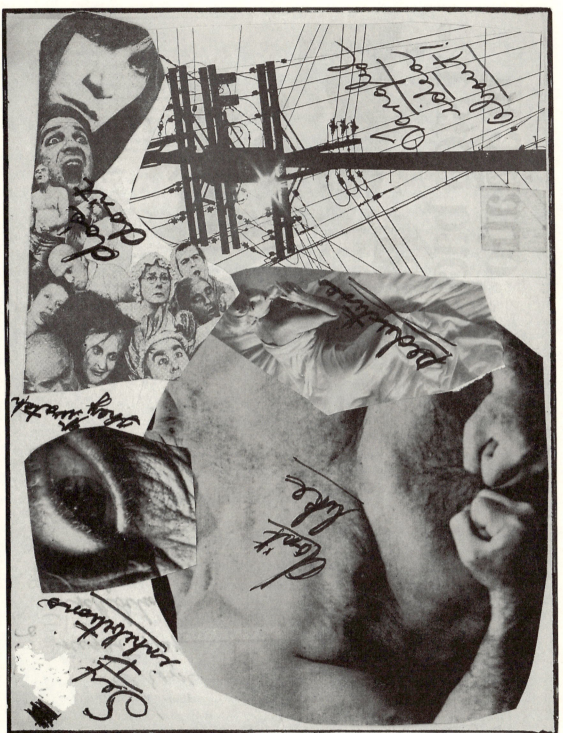

FIGURE 22E

Black 41-Year-Old Male: Role Reversal

Trayvis Brown was a highly successful attorney. His father had died suddenly when Trayvis was five, leaving his mother to raise him. The presenting problem was an inability to sustain a lasting relationship with a woman. Although he found the women he dated "great" at first, everything would "go sour" about six months later.

During the developmental history, Trayvis mentioned that his mother often made him angry and irritable. He was beginning to wonder if his feelings toward her somehow got in the way of how he felt about other women.

After several months of therapy, the client began to recognize a behavioral pattern. After he spent time with his mother he tended to have an argument with his girlfriend, Francene. Recently, she had complained that Trayvis was "picking" on her without reason. He was upset since he had been considering marriage with Francene.

During one therapy session, Trayvis was directed: *Make a collage about your mother. Include what you like and don't like about her.* The completed MPC showed nine positive images, with only two minor complaints. Assessing this fact, he said, "I don't know what she does wrong. She just drives me nuts." Even when he questioned WHY she bothered him, he was unable to respond.

It was when Trayvis was told to *pick out a few pictures and then to free associate to them* that a subtle but major clue was presented. The *telling hint* was unconsciously hidden in a bland looking picture and is an example of how a single picture in an MPC can make an impact on the therapy. The MPC (Figure 23A) contained:

1. *A black man in graduation cap and gown* was thinking, "I've come a long way baby."
2. *A Black baby holding a spoon to his mother's mouth* was associated with, "The mother is trying to feed her baby, but instead the little boy is feeding her."
3. *Black figures of an older couple, a middle-aged woman, and a young woman* were identified as, "two grandparents, a mother and a daughter."
4. *A Black woman* was noted as, "a happy person, because she likes her job."

The significant image in this MPC was the second one, of the *child feeding his parent.* A role reversal seemed plausible. This dynamic is often present with little boys who are raised in a single-parent household.

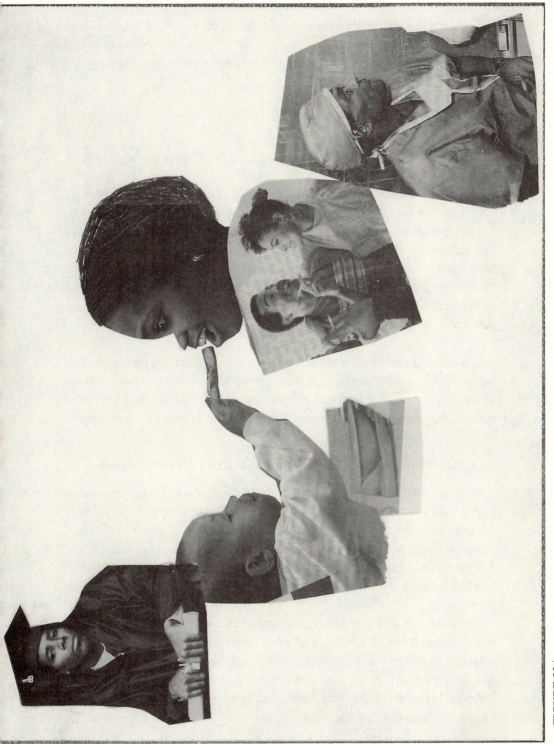

FIGURE 23A

To enable this possibility to be explored, the therapist told the client: *Create a collage that shows the messages you received as a child from the adults around you.* Trayvis was thoughtful and very involved in making a careful pictorial search for this topic.

The MPC (Figure 23B) included:

1. *A small Black boy.*
2. *A Black man's portrait.* This was superimposed over the boy's face.

As Trayis examined the collage, he fell sadly silent. Then overwhelmed by his insight, he began to tear. The tears he shed were for his lost childhood.

The perception that he had "forever" been responsible for his mother made him furious. He recalled that over and over again well meaning relatives told him, "Now, Trayvis, with your father gone, you are the man of the house."

Although the client always knew that his mother was a very capable person and parent, he believed it was up to him to take care of her. This conviction, inculcated at the age of five, clung to him still.

Comments. In subsequent sessions, Trayvis recognized his perception that women were dependent and men were totally responsible for them. His resentment over his self-imposed role of "caretaker" had blocked him from sustaining a serious relationship and making a commitment to a woman.

Caucasian 45-Year-Old Female: Borderline Personality

Amy was originally seen in therapy with her eight-year-old daughter because of the child's behavioral problems. Proud of her career progress as a fabric designer she wanted to start her own business.

During an interview, she happened to mention that jobs were changed often. Although Amy quit some firms, she was fired from others. The last position was lost because she was caught taking fabric home without her employer's permission.

The client was proud of her regular attendance at Alcoholics Anonymous and of the fact that she had been "sober" for three years. Since Amy had parenting problems, she was assigned to a Single Parents Group. Her daughter was referred to a Latency Age Group for boys and girls.

Amy's MPCs from the third, fifth, and sixth week in group therapy are reported below.

FIGURE 23B

Third Week

During the third group meeting, Amy described her feelings of detachment. In an attempt to grasp a better picture of her disengagement, the therapist told the entire group: *Create a collage that shows WHO YOU ARE.*

Amy's MPC (Figure 24A) included:

1. *A Caucasian woman holding a deck of cards.* It meant, "I'm learning to be good at this game just like my new best friend."
2. *A window* was drawn in by Amy.
3. *A woman's face with the eyes, nose, and mouth removed* represented, "This is my last therapist, I thought I was a lot like her, but when I saw how selfish she was I realized we had nothing in common. Now I have a new friend. We have lots in common and I know what she is thinking."

Comments. The MPC had strong clues to Amy's questionable sense of self. It also hinted at a tendency to fuse with other persons, which, with the over-attachment and then disengagement, suggested the possibility of a Borderline Personality.

Fifth Week

During the fifth session, the group's instructions were: *Pick out ONE picture, either of a person or a miscellaneous item, and paste it onto the page. It will be discussed in group.*

Amy was unable to contain herself when she reached into other people's boxes and took out a fistful of pictures. Instead of one picture, she pasted down two.

Amy's MPC (Figure 24B) included:

1. *Three people emerging through Venetian blinds.* Amy told the group, "I just picked out this picture because I thought it was interesting, but it doesn't really seem to have any real meaning for me."
2. *A person in a box that recedes back into space* brought the remark, "That's how I feel sometimes, like there's a lot of distance that I feel."

Comments. The images of the *emerging bodies* exhibited Amy's feelings that she lacked substance, while the *boxed-in person* exemplified her distanced experience. These points strengthened the possible Borderline diagnosis.

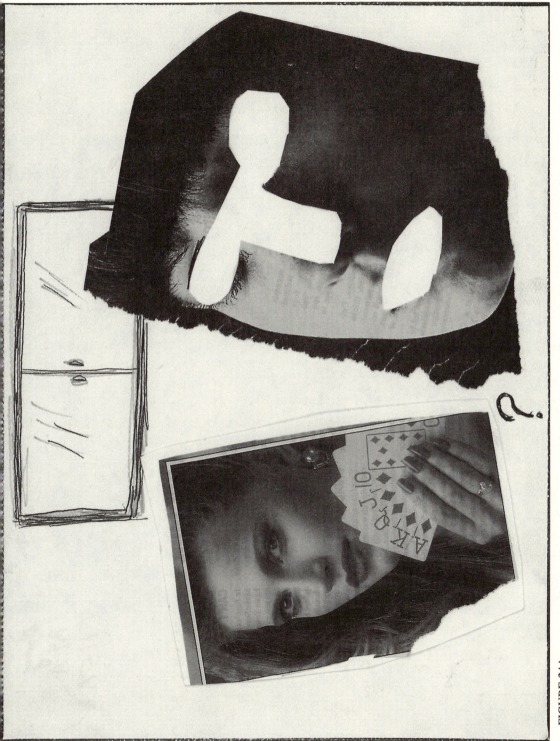

FIGURE 24A

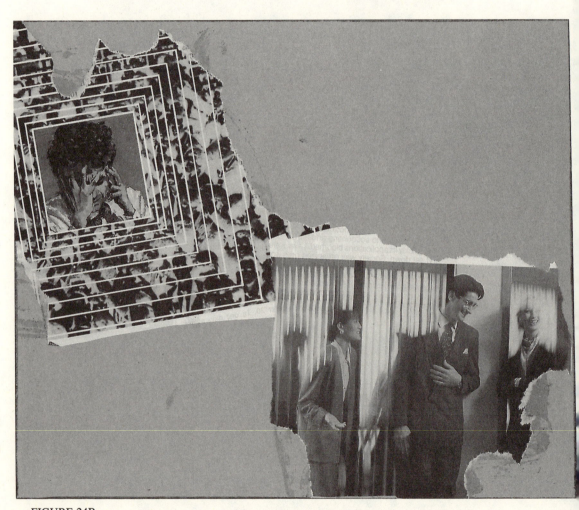

FIGURE 24B

Sixth Week

For the sixth session, the group's instructions were: *Pick out pictures that show HOW YOU SEE YOURSELF.*

Amy's MPC (figure not shown) included:

1. *A woman's figure repeated five times, with each figure less defined as it goes farther back into space,* illustrated, "Sometimes, I feel like I'm going to disappear."
2. *A woman looking at her reflection in a window* was explained, "Sometimes it seems that I'm looking at myself through a window, sort of like I am able to see myself from far away. It's a weird feeling."

Comments. Amy's MPCs demonstrated a dissolution of the self. Along with the information received at the interview it validated the Borderline assessment.

The members of the group did not realize the significance of her collage. They projected their own experiences onto it. For example, Jennie, an obese woman, talked about the day she unexpectedly came upon a mirror and was surprised to see how big she really was. She confessed that she had still thought about herself as thin.

Shirley added how upset she was each morning when she had to confront her age, in spite of her internal youthful image. Other participants also agreed that their mind's-eye impression differed from the one reflected in the mirror.

Caucasian Family: Perceptions of Family Members

Patrick McGregor, a Caucasian 13-year-old boy, was the designated patient. His parents described him as oppositional and uncooperative in fulfilling household responsibilities. Mr. and Mrs. McGregor were tired of nagging their son and getting no results. They told the therapist they wanted their "kid fixed."

In contrast, outside the home Patrick's behavior brought him popularity with peers and successful school performance.

When seen alone, he was certain that the therapist would "side" with his parents. Regardless, he condescended to answer the interview questions and agreed to a family meeting with his parents and sister Shelley.

A family session displayed his father's poor communication. He avoided Patrick's appropriate confrontations and complaints. A mild-mannered person, he was polite, yet the answers he gave were not direct. This had a frustrating effect on Patrick, but did not bother his wife or daughter.

After several sessions, it was evident that Mr. McGregor was unaware of the role he played in the family system. As an aid in helping him gain insight, the family was instructed: *Pick out pictures from the MISCELLANEOUS ITEMS to describe how you see each member of your family, include yourself. Use ONE PAGE for EACH PERSON.*

When the family got started, Patrick insisted Shelley's pictures were better than his. Without permission, he exchanged their boxes. Mr. Mc Gregor was the first to finish and left the table to look around the office.

The parents' perceptions of Patrick matched their complaints, while Shelley showed him to be "nice" and "strong, too." Patrick presented himself as a "good student, good athlete and popular with peers."

Everyone showed SHELLEY as "cute" and "sweet." Her self-perception was, "a good dancer, and with lots of friends."

MOTHER was seen by everyone, including herself, as "organized," and Patrick added a "nagging" dimension.

Mr. McGregor's collage (Figure 25A) about himself displayed a person who: "loves his wife and his family, enjoys fishing, can clown around, is hard-working and likes his job."

Thus far, there were no surprises. But when Patrick's father viewed the others' perception of him, he was stunned. Mrs. McGregor's collage (Figure 25B) included most of what her husband had shared. However, she also included the "big worrier" part that is concerned with money and work. Mr. McGregor admitted this was "true."

Shelley represented her father through a "teddy bear" and someone she "loved" (Figure 25C). Although this was intended as a compliment, the father realized that a "teddy bear was cuddly," but it did not show him as an effective parent.

It was Patrick's MPC (Figure 25D), so graphically clear, that hurt his father deeply. He was portrayed through the image of a *man with a camera for a face, wearing blinders made of money.* The third and most painful statement was *two mountain climbers—the man was reaching out to pull the boy up,* but as Patrick explained it, "the man never quite reaches the boy." "Dad has good intentions," Patrick added, "but he can never take time out from work for me."

When Mr. McGregor asked for examples, Patrick gave him a list. It made his father feel very sad, but he realized the truth in what his son said.

Comments. This technique helped to reach Mr. McGregor's awareness. It was impossible to ignore his chidren's visual statements. This session made an impact upon Patrick's father. He began to put effort into being a more active parent.

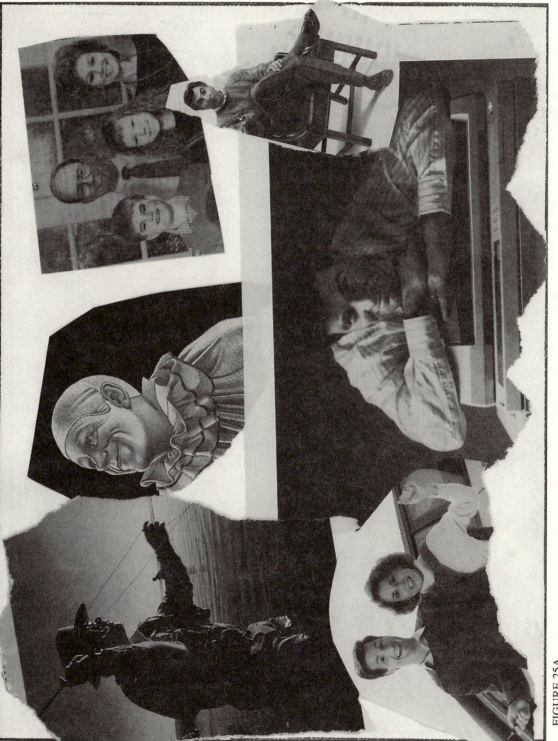

FIGURE 25A

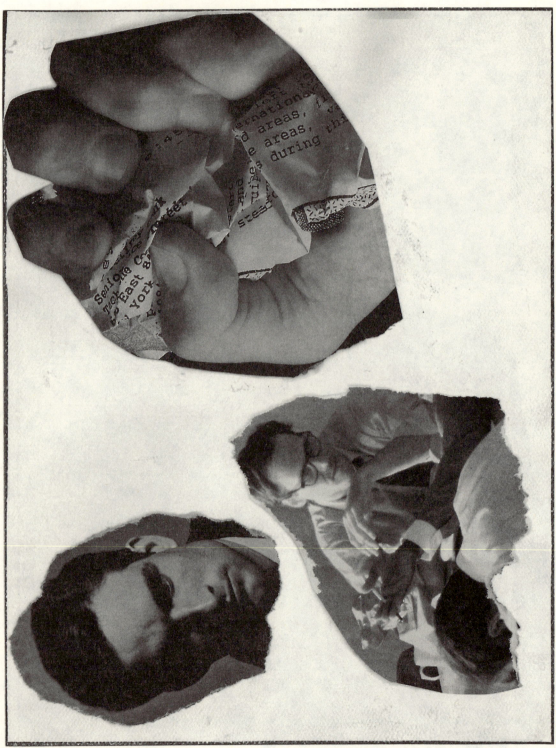

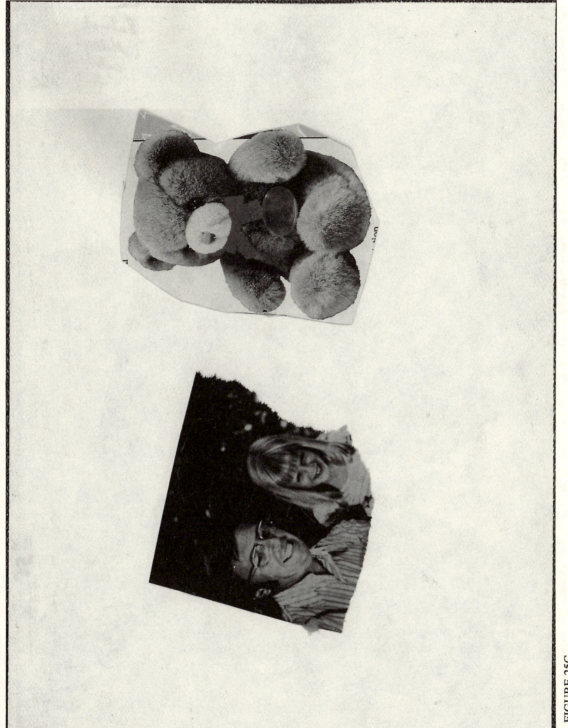

FIGURE 25C

FIGURE 25D

Asian 83-Year-Old Female: Positive Life Review

Mrs. Wada was an attractive Japanese woman in the upper socioeconomic level. She lived in a luxurious retirement apartment. She had seven children and many grandchildren and great grandchildren. Depressed since her husband died several years ago, she obsessively ruminated on her past hardships. Her children wanted to fulfil their filial responsibilities, but their mother's rancor exasperated and infuriated them. Pained by the dilemma, they sought geriatric therapy for their parent.

During the interview, Mrs. Wada listed numerous complaints. Many of them were valid. However, pessimism took over all her thoughts. When questioned about her past, she talked only about the difficult times that she had lived through. The horrendous ordeal of the Japanese internment camp in California during World War II was told in detail. She berated her family, flipping back and forth between their early childhood and the present time.

First Through Third Weeks

To get the client away from her obsessive ruminations, the therapist applied the MPC technique. The box of people pictures was mainly filled with images of Japanese individuals. In the belief that a POSITIVE LIFE REVIEW would be helpful, Mrs. Wada was instructed: *Pick out pictures of people that stand for persons in your past who have given you pleasure.*

The client thought this was a childish pursuit. Regardless, when the many Japanese people pictures were noticed, she began the task. Mrs. Wada allowed herself the comfort of remembering loved ones. She became so absorbed that she ended up with six different MPCs on this same subject. They referred mainly to individuals from her distant past. A typical MPC (Figure 26A) included these elements:

1. *A young Asian girl* reminded her, "When I was young I was really beautiful."
2. *A young Asian woman in traditional clothes* was identified as, "This is something like my sister. She died when she was very young, many years ago."
3. *A young Asian man* symbolized "my older brother. We were very close. When some of my family came to the United States, he didn't want to come because of his wife, who wouldn't leave her family."

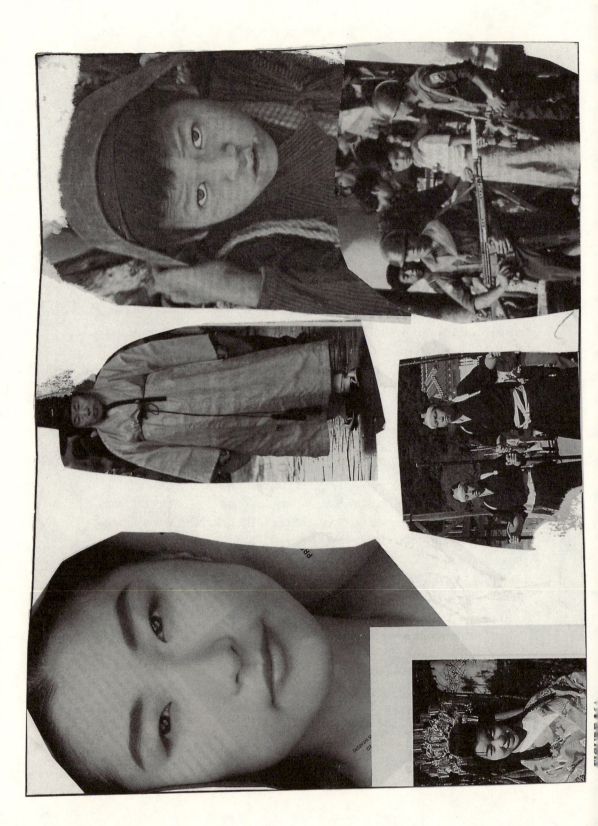

4. *An old Asian man in traditional garb* was a reminder of "my grandfather who I loved very much. He never came to America."
5. *A little Asian boy carrying a pack on his back* brought back the memory of, "my younger brother who died a couple of years ago. He came to America with me."
6. *A soldier* brought her sadness. She stated, "this is like my nephew who was killed in the big war. He was the son of my sister that I showed you."

Comments. Mrs. Wada found the experience engaging. It was worthwhile because by sharing her past her present worth was validated.

Fourth Through Eighth Weeks

By the time the sixth session took place, the subject of *people who are remembered with pleasure* was exhausted. The client was ready to turn to a new theme. Mrs. Wada became dedicated to the next task. It required her to *make a collage that shows any kind of JOYFUL memories that you have. They can be about events in your life, things that you had, or any other positive remembrances.*

Comments. The topic of "reminiscing positive memories" was repeated in the seventh and eighth sessions. The pictures were used as a catalyst to help her recollect the favorable parts of her life. This technique stimulated the revival of other satisfactory situations.

Ninth Week

Fully acquainted with the MPC procedure, Mrs. Wada was encouraged to select her own topic. Instead of choosing a subject first, she began by rummaging through the photographs in the box of miscellaneous items. She became attracted to several vividly colored photographs and decided to paste them down. As she did so, Mrs. Wada talked about the memories that were evoked (Figure 26B).

The MPC included:

1. *Vegetables* prompted her to talk about the garden that she and her husband had tended. She was happy to report how much they enjoyed eating the vegetables they grew.
2. *Car keys* suggested the Sunday rides that the family took to the park, flower gardens, or just along the beach. Sometimes they visited relatives.
3. A *bridge* acted as a stimulus to talk about the time she and her family lived in San Francisco.

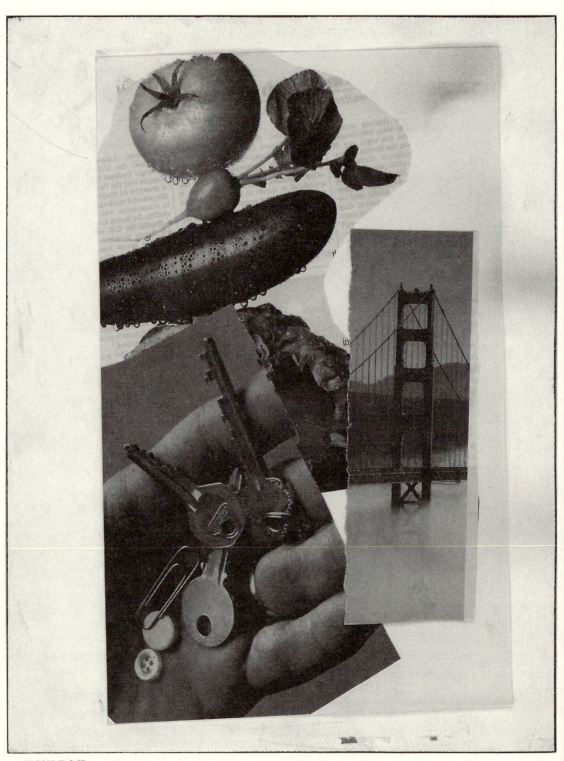

FIGURE 26B

When the therapy session was finishing, Mrs. Wada said she was disappointed because her collage was unfinished. Consequently, it was decided that she would continue in the next meeting.

Tenth–Eleventh Weeks

At the beginning of the meeting, the client admitted that she looked forward to finishing her "series" of POSITIVE MEMORIES. Rather than continuing to work on the collage from the last session, she decided to begin anew. Mrs. Wada requested a new piece of paper, the collage boxes, and the other supplies.

In a short time, she discovered two photos, one of a *briefcase* and the other of the *Buddha* (Figure 26C). Together, these pictures stood for the export business that she and her husband had operated.

Many tales were spun off from this topic. She recapitulated the story of their business, from how it got started to the way they bought their art objects to the eventual success that she and her husband shared. She even talked about certain customers and the type of commercial relationships that they had.

Although this subject took up almost the entire session, Mrs. Wada insisted on talking about a particular picture of an *adult holding the hand of a child*. She explained that it represented her children and grandchildren to whom the business was given (Figure 26D).

Because the MPC mode was so successful, it was continued with a variety of subjects. For instance, the directive to *create a collage about the relatives in your life who have made you proud or have given you happiness,* was used several times. While she tried to master these tasks, she was surprised to discover so many satisfying metaphoric photos. All of the images are of Asian people.

The MPC (Figure 26E) included:

1. *A sleeping child* reminded her of a great grandchild who was so much like her own son, when he was little.
2-3. *Baseball players* represented many of her grandchildren who were good in sports.
4. The *teacher* illustrated her grandchildren who were educators.
5. *A female dentist* was similar to a great granddaughter who was a dental hygienist.
6. *A medical doctor* was like one of her grandsons.
7. The *woman on the phone* symbolized a granddaughter who ran a successful business.

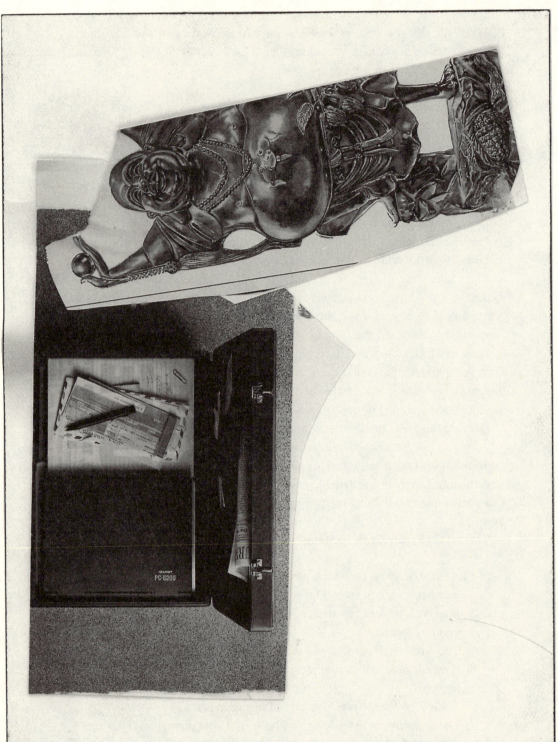

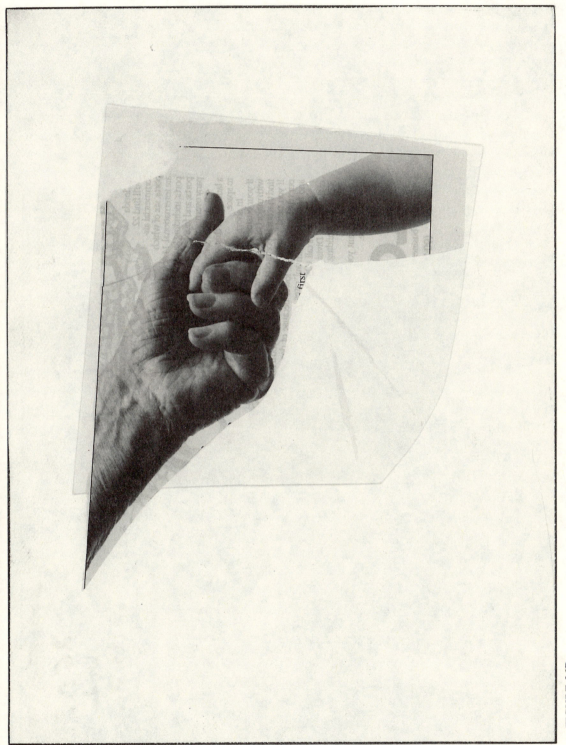

FIGURE 26D

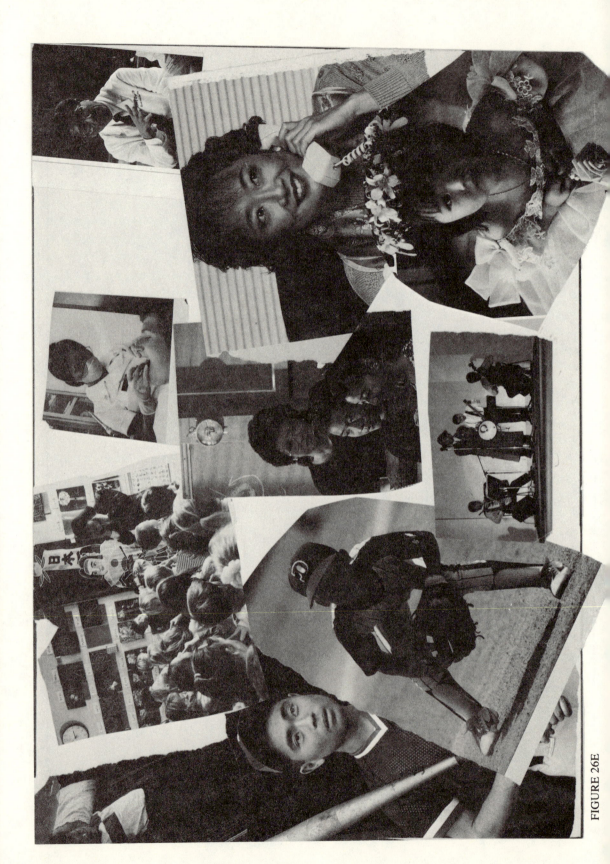

FIGURE 26E

8. *A woman with two children* was a metaphor for her granddaughter who was a *school psychologist*.
9. *Musicians* represented family members who played various instruments.
10. *A child dressed up in fancy clothes* was a reminder that one of her great grandchildren had recently been a flower girl at a family wedding.

Because Mrs. Wada was so positively engrossed in the MPC, she was told to do *homework*. She was encouraged to continue to make collages *on her own*, then to bring them to the sessions to be shared. When she agreed, the collage materials were handed over to her to use at home.

This tactic would serve as a transitional object and would help her to be independently creative.

Twelfth Through Fourteenth Weeks

After Mrs. Wada worked on her collages at home, she acknowledged, "It helps to pass the time away." She notified the therapist that she was collecting pictures from her own Japanese magazines and newspapers to use for her collages. She added they were "much better" then those supplied by the therapist.

With the client's consent, a family session was planned. Beforehand, it was suggested that some of her collages be shown during that meeting. The goal was to use the collages as a focus on the positive aspects of this matriarch's life. It was hoped that the family would enjoy the MPCs and would be motivated toward constructive communication.

Fifteenth Week

The Wada family was gladdened to see their matriarch's creations and to hear their meanings. They were astonished by the wealth of her productions. Seeing all of the positive memories brought them pride and satisfaction. Many questions were asked of their mother and she was pleased with their interest.

Although she managed to throw in complaints about her children, they did not mind since it was in the midst of a positive atmosphere.

The intimacy that the family experienced was one that they had forgotten; its renewal lifted their spirits. Mrs. Wada was exhausted but happy for the attention she received when the session ended.

Comments. The meeting had an effect on the Wada children. They were captivated by the way their mother had creatively delineated her wealth of experiences. Though much of the information was not new, it reminded them that their mother deserved their respect and admiration. The family session made a warm impression upon Mrs. Wada. She recognized that once again she was being seen as the venerated elder.

References

Constantino, G., Malgady, R. G., & Rogler, L. H. (1988). *TEMAS (Tell Me A Story) Manual.* Los Angeles: Western Psychological Services.

Murray, H. A. (1943). *Thematic Apperception Test.* Cambridge, MA: Harvard University Press.

Culturally Slanted Magazine Publications

The magazines listed below are not recommended for article content. They are listed due to their ethnic imagery.

INTERNATIONAL

Faces International. 10537 Santa Monica Blvd., Los Angeles, CA 90025.
Family Circle. U.S. Route 45, North Mattoon, IL 61938.
Money. P.O. Box 617901, Tampa, FL 33661-1790.
Parenting. 301 Howard St. (17th Floor), San Francisco, CA 94105.
World Monitor. P.O. Box 11267, Des Moines, IA 50347-1267.

ASIAN*

Asian Pacific Travel. 1540 Gilbreth Road, Burlingame, CA 94010.
Asiaweek. Asiaweek Limited c/o Expediters of the Printed Word Ltd., 2323 Randolph Ave., Avenel, NJ 07001.
Dongnai. P.O. Box 2318, Westminister, CA 92683. (A gratis Vietnamese paper).
Khoe Dep. Fax: (714) 537-4986. (A gratis Vietnamese paper.)
Far Eastern Economic Review. Review Publishing Company Limited, c/o DKL, 240 Valley Drive, Brisbane, CA 94005.
Nang. 13876 Brookhurst St., Garden Grove, CA 92643. (A gratis Vietnamese paper.)
Transpacific! c/o TMI Subscriptions, 23715 W. Malibu Road, No. 390, Malibu, CA 90265-9986.

BLACK

Africa Report. P.O. Box 3000, Dept. AR, Denville, NJ 07834.
Black Enterprise. P.O. Box 3011, Harlan, IA 51593-2101.
Ebony. P.O. Box 690, Chicago, IL 60690-9983.
EM: Ebony Man. P.O. Box 549, Chicago, IL 60690-9983.

*Japanese language magazines on a large variety of subjects are flown in daily from Japan. For information or orders phone Tama Book Store (310) 477-8686.

Essence. P.O. Box 51300, Boulder, CO 80321-1300.
Jet. P.O. Box 538, Chicago, IL 60690.
Upscale. P.O. Box 10798, Atlanta, GA 30357-9836.
Yo. P.O. Box 88427, Los Angeles, CA 90009.

HISPANIC**

Esto. Organizacion, Editorial Mexican, Mario Vazquez Rana, Mexico, D. F., Viernes 5. Mexico.
Hispanic. 111 Massachusetts Ave., N.W. (suite 410), Washington, D.C. 20077-0253.
Mi Casa. Viva America Media Group. 1645 No. Vine St. #200, Hollywood, CA 90028. (A gratis publication.)
Prensa Libre. 13 Calle 9-31, Zona 1, Guatemala, Central America.
TV y Novelas. P.O. Box 230, Miami, FL 3316.

INDIANS (of the Americas)

Report on the Americas. NACLA, 475 Riverside Dr., Suite 454, New York, NY 10115.

**Many Hispanic magazines are translations of popular English language publications such as Redbook, Time, and so on. The articles and ads in these magazines are not focused on Hispanic persons.

Index